X *thai* ___

"Kristin Carmichael has simplified the amazingly complex subject of how to leave a bad man or difficult relationship. Not an easy task in our culture, which suggests that a big part of a woman's identity is created by her intimate relationship. With compassion, humor, and a straightforward writing style, Kristin delivers real solutions for real women facing difficult relationship problems. She empowers her readers by suggesting that all women deserve fulfilling, mutually beneficial, loving, and respectful intimate relationships."

— Noël Bridget Busch-Armendariz, PhD, LMSW, MPA
Associate Professor and Director,
The University of Texas at Austin School of Social Work

"Recognizing that coercive control merely changes its form when women leave abusive men, *X That Ex* offers a step-by-step guide to resistance and survival. Realistic without being depressing, educational without being patronizing, this is an invaluable compendium of practical advice, case examples, encouragement, and wisdom that belongs on your kitchen table, not on the shelf."

— Evan Stark, PhD, MSW
Author of *Coercive Control* and
Professor Emeritus, Rutgers University

"Simply brilliant. Expertly written by someone with a deep caring and understanding of this very complex issue. For the thousands (or millions) who continue to be hurt by their Exes, this book offers a useful and compassionate guide. For professionals dedicated to supporting women who have been through destructive relationships, this book is a must-have for the tool box."

— Kathy Armijo-Etre, PhD, Vice President, Community Health,
CHRISTUS St. Vincent Regional Medical Center

"Where was this book 30 years ago? Finally a book that informs and empowers women who may be on the fence about their decision, or who struggle emotionally, to stay away from a manipulative Ex. Thank you, Kristin, for writing a book that I would recommend to everyone; a book that will no doubt change lives."

— Peggy Luplow, Development Fundraiser,
Esperanza Shelter for Battered Families, Inc.

"It's not enough to know the signs of a bad relationship in order to leave one. With skill and care, Kristin makes sense of a tumultuous and emotional time and gives readers concrete tools to understand the tactics manipulative Exes use and how to defend against them."

— Alena Schaim, Executive Director and Instructor,
IMPACT Personal Safety

"The perfect book for someone leaving an Ex they can't seem to shake. Get ready to be amazed by how much you never knew about manipulative Exes and the power you have to free yourself from them."

— Mary Justice, Director, Care Connection,
CHRISTUS St. Vincent Regional Medical Center

◄ DEDICATION ►

To Henry M. Lopez —
A man who loves his family,
a well-told story, diet soda,
the "Pigeon," and super-geeky sci-fi.
I love you in this dimension and every other.

Ordering
Trade bookstores in the U.S. and Canada please contact:

Publishers Group West
1700 Fourth Street, Berkeley CA 94710
Phone: (800) 788-3123   Fax: (800) 351-5073

For bulk orders please contact:
Special Sales
Hunter House Inc., PO Box 2914, Alameda CA 94501-0914
Phone: (510) 899-5041   Fax: (510) 865-4295
E-mail: sales@hunterhouse.com

Individuals can order our books by calling (800) 266-5592
or from our website at **www.hunterhouse.com**

X that Ex

**MAKING A CLEAN BREAK
WHEN THE RELATIONSHIP IS OVER**

Best Wishes

Kristin E. Carmichael, LISW

Hunter House
PUBLISHERS

Hunter House Inc., Publishers
PO Box 2914
Alameda CA 94501-0914

Library of Congress Cataloging-in-Publication Data
Carmichael, Kristin E.
X that ex : making a clean break when the relationship is over /
Kristin E. Carmichael.
p. cm.
Includes index.
ISBN 978-0-89793-640-8 (pbk.)
1. Man-woman relationships—Psychological aspects. 2. Separation
(Psychology) 3. Women—Psychology. 4. Interpersonal relations—
Psychological aspects. 5. Interpersonal conflict. I. Title.
HQ801.C283 2012
306.89—dc23   2012030705

Project Credits

Cover Design: Brian Dittmar Design, Inc.
Book Production: John McKercher
Developmental Editor: Jude Berman
Copy Editor: Kelley Blewster
Proofreader: Martha Scarpati
Indexer: Candace Hyatt
Managing Editor: Alexandra Mummery
Acquisitions Assistant: Elana Fiske

Editorial Intern: Tu-Anh Dang-Tran
Special Sales Manager: Judy Hardin
Rights Coordinator: Candace Groskreutz
Customer Service Manager:
Christina Sverdrup
Order Fulfillment: Washul Lakdhon
Administrator: Theresa Nelson
Computer Support: Peter Eichelberger
Publisher: Kiran S. Rana

Printed and bound by Sheridan Books, Ann Arbor, Michigan
Manufactured in the United States of America

9 8 7 6 5 4 3 2 1   First Edition   12 13 14 15 16

Contents

Part I: Your Ex's Playbook

Part II: Surefire Strategies for X-ing Your Ex

◀ ▶

For more information about the book and its author,
to sign up for support and information by e-mail,
and for notification of the author's seminars
and lectures, visit **XThatEx.com.**

Important Note

The material in this book is intended to help women end destructive or dangerous relationships. Every effort has been made to provide accurate and dependable information. The contents of this book have been compiled through professional research and in consultation with other mental-health specialists. However, the reader should be aware that professionals in the field have differing opinions.

Therefore, the publisher, author, and editors, as well as the professionals quoted in the book, cannot be held responsible for any error, omission, or dated material. The author and publisher assume no responsibility for any outcome of applying the information in this book in a program of self-care or under the care of a licensed practitioner. If you have questions concerning your relationships, or about the application of the information described in this book, consult a qualified mental-health professional. If you are in a violent or potentially violent relationship or have any questions about abuse of any kind, please call a domestic-abuse hotline.

Acknowledgments

My deepest gratitude to:

The courageous women at CHRISTUS St. Vincent Regional Medical Center and Esperanza Shelter for Battered Families Inc., who have trusted and shared their stories with me; my family, especially Henry M. Lopez, Dawn Carmichael, and Sue Henry, who have been invaluable supports to my writing; influential colleagues and friends Kathy Armijo-Etre, Mary Justice, Jeannette Baca, Julio Cervantes, Pam Wiseman, Virginia Griffey, Alena Schaim, Trasie Topple, Sara Hope Franks, Kathryn Ugoretz, and Karen Gano; my lovely group of girlfriends and Nomi Green, I am so lucky to have you in my life; members of the hard-working Domestic Violence Design Team and the Medical Action Team; and my sweet pound puppies and kitties.

Thanks also to everyone at Hunter House Publishers, with special recognition of publisher Kiran Rana and editor Kelley Blewster for taking this book from good to great.

Although the stories in this book are true, I have respected a number of the contributors' requests to remain anonymous or to be identified by pseudonyms.

Introduction

So you left a bad man.

He was obviously not *completely* bad, but he was no good for you.

He may have been a control freak, drama king, alcoholic, workaholic, rage-a-holic, egomaniac, love withholder, or any other term that describes a guy who definitely isn't able to give you what you deserve. I have no idea how you left, but it must have been hell. Leaving someone who treated you crappy or worse, who you in some way fear, is a really big deal. And by doing so, you are one step closer to having the life you were meant for.

I wish all women who have done what you did would be rewarded with a month on the beach in Tahiti. Then we could soak up the sun, heal our wounds, revel in our amazing courage and intelligence, and rediscover the beauty in the world. Only after this I-left-a-jerk holiday would we come back to the real world, refreshed and ready for whatever tricks our Ex has cooked up.

Barring the chance that you have the time and money to take such a trip, now is not when you should let down your guard. You must prepare to stay away from him. And staying away for good can be incredibly difficult.

You are probably feeling a mix of emotions: overwhelmed, happy, sad, fearful, lonely, and, hopefully, free. This may not be the first time you have left. You may be second-guessing your decision, or you may feel very confident about what you have done. Either way, odds are you're wondering what he will do next and how it will affect you.

You do not need to be a psychic to know what a bad or even an abusive man will do when you leave him. You just need to have some experience with the situation or access to someone who does. And since most people don't leave relationships every day, this knowledge can be hard to come by. Lots of friends and family members may give you advice during this time. As much as they may be trying to help, most of them don't have any more knowledge about the scenario than you do.

I have worked with thousands of women who were trying to leave and stay gone from bad relationships. This experience has given me the opportunity to see over and over again the tactics used by Exes who are determined to get back at their partners and to get their partners back. I will pass this vital information on to you. If there is one thing I have learned, it is that continued pain, confusion, fear, and ultimately returning to your Ex are not inevitable. There are certain strategies that when put to work can dramatically increase your odds for success. This book will reveal those techniques to you. It will help you avoid your Ex's traps, help you protect yourself emotionally, and, most of all, help you to stay gone.

Although this book is written to reflect a heterosexual relationship wherein a woman has left her male partner, in my experience the struggle to stay free from a hurtful Ex is not something that only women go through. It is a human challenge that can be experienced by women and men of all cultures, ethnicities, races, sexualities, religions, ages, and economic levels. By and large, the information provided in this book can be used when ending a same-sex relationship, when a man is struggling with the temptation to return to a female partner, or even in negative relationships with family members or ex-friends from whom you want to distance yourself.

How This Book Is Different

Many books will tell you how to spot and sidestep the wrong person for a relationship. Others will tell you how to get out of a dysfunctional relationship. Still others will try to help you heal from what you have been through. All are worthy topics.

But none (until now!) are solely devoted to helping you make good decisions during that crucial period right after you have left your partner. Life can be really tough post-breakup, and it is then that many good, smart, strong women return to bad relationships over and over. It's not because they aren't trying hard. It is because they haven't been taught how to do this thing, this leaving for good. They haven't been shown how to pack away years or months of emotion, connection, shared experiences, and hopes that things would get better. After all, women are usually the peacemakers and relationship-builders, so we often have to go through a process of trial and error to leave permanently. Sadly, some of us never "get it right"—never get to live free of a partner who hurts us.

It is hugely important to recognize that many people, and perhaps the majority of women, will be lulled into dating or marrying at least one not-so-good guy at some point in their lives. How many women do you know who never went on a date with a person who turned out to be a real creep? And we all know that real creeps cannot be relied on to leave when they see that they are making us miserable. That means a significant amount of our happiness depends not only on leaving people who are bad for us, but also on our ability to move on from those relationships to something else—hopefully to something else that is much more healthy and fulfilling.

If a woman cannot find it within herself to move on and stay gone, she is just as trapped as if she had never left—maybe even more so—and she will always be at the mercy of self-centered men who do not value her or treat her the way she deserves. That is hardly the future little girls dream of.

In all the time I played with dolls as a kid, Ken never called Barbie names, yelled, made her feel bad about herself, or tore up the mansion. He just cruised around in *her* convertible looking fly. That was his job. Of course, the job of human males is much more complex, and certainly there may be times when they lose their tempers or are a pain to be around. No one is perfect. But you and I both know that there is a line that once crossed cannot be uncrossed. A line beyond which your partner can irrevocably change from a loving Ken with some issues to Not the Person I Should Be With. It can happen with a slap or, less dramatically but equally painfully, with his being too controlling, withholding love, not accepting or respecting you for who you are, or only caring for himself. And if this shift happens, no matter how it happens, you will have some big, tough decisions to make. Perhaps the biggest one is when and how to leave.

Have you ever noticed that there is never a good time to leave the person you are with? It is *always* his birthday, the day his loved one passed away, Christmas, Valentine's Day, your anniversary, a Monday and you are too tired, a Friday and you are going out of town, a Wednesday and he is acting particularly unstable, etc., etc., etc. In my opinion there is *one* day each year when you can conveniently break it off: March 8th, which happens to be National Women's Day. It's well past the holiday season, not too hot, not too cold, hopefully no one's birthday. Your act of self-preservation on this day can serve as a salute to women everywhere who do what they have to do to live happily and be true to themselves. All in all, it's a pretty good day for a dumping.

Of course, if you were to miss March 8th you would have to take your chances on finding another day conducive to breaking up and may just end up putting it off. I am definitely against that scenario. Whatever date you choose, I am glad you are reading this book now. That tells me you must have figured out how and when to get out, because you are already on to the next challenge—staying gone.

Do the Math

There are plenty of creeps out there. A certain number of them are your average but still harmful Garden Variety Creeps; others are the more destructive mind-warping Super Creeps; a few are the very dangerous Super-Evil-Psycho Creeps. Even though only a small percentage of the male population has earned one of these designations, this still means big trouble for *all* of us gals. Because throughout their days on the planet, from age fifteen to seventy-five, these creeps will be trolling the dating waters looking for the big-hearted, the beautiful, and often the injured and vulnerable among us. You may be feeling pretty good about yourself and the way your life is going (or not), may have had happy experiences growing up (or not), may have a solid idea of what you want in a relationship (or not). Whatever your circumstances, you're not completely immune to the attentions of a creep. Sometimes a creep will pick a woman who has dated other creeps and sometimes not. But once he finds his unlucky prey, a creep will always strategically seduce her and usually will stay with her for as long as she can be convinced to put up with his bad behavior. Oh, and as an added bonus, his poor behavior tends to get worse over time. Not a very pretty picture, especially if you are the one he is professing to love. Throughout their dating careers, these men can negatively impact the lives of dozens of women before they are done causing havoc. If we do the math, we can see that the relatively small percentage of screwed-up men in America, multiplied by the number of women they date or marry in their lifetimes, equals a mega-ton of trouble.

There is a good chance you will run across one of these guys; in fact, I don't know too many women who haven't been in your situation at some point in their lives. The formula for surviving a run-in with a creep is this:

A. If you see one coming, listen to your instincts and run, don't walk, the other way.

B. If you do get into a relationship with him, you are going to have to leave it.

C. Once you are out of the relationship, you have got to stay free of it.

This book is geared to helping you with step C—staying free. The most crucial information for you to learn in order to accomplish your goal of staying away is to understand your Ex's playbook of strategies (Part I of this book) and how to neutralize them (Part II). I use the metaphor of a playbook because I think it is important to remember that many of the things he may say or do in an effort to get you to come back to him are to some degree calculated. They are done from a place of strategy, not love. Just like in sports, every play your Ex makes may further his goal of encroaching on your emotional territory, your kindness, your attention, your hope, or your fears. I want to make it clear that I am not using the concept of a playbook because I think in any way that what you are going through is a sport. Quite the contrary. I know full well that staying away from your Ex is no game and that it may in fact determine your happiness, your well-being, and for some women, even their safety.

Who This Book Is For

X That Ex is intended for readers who have had a broad range of experiences—from women who have left men who were just not so good to them, to women who have left clearly abusive men. What this means is that some of the information contained in this book will resonate with you and some won't. I encourage you to continue reading even if you come across information that does not seem to apply to your situation. More than likely, within a few sentences or paragraphs, you will again encounter material that is targeted to helping someone in your situation.

Please also keep in mind that just because your Ex may not engage in some of the more dramatic or obviously hurtful ploys described here does not mean that this book cannot assist you, or that you should consider your Ex as being "not so bad." Even though some tactics may be more harmful in certain ways than others, none of the behaviors I depict are nice things for Exes to do, and they all have the power to derail your plans for continued separation. As you read, think hard to see if each tactic might apply to your situation. But know, thankfully, that *not all will*. Almost all hurtful Exes will pick a handful of strategies and use them over and over.

I've listed in the early chapters direct quotes from Exes who attempted to manipulate their former partners. I gathered these quotes over a number of years from women who were in situations like yours. Your Ex may use the same words their Exes did, or he may pick different ones to convey the same meaning. I hope these quotes can make the concepts in the book come alive and feel more real to you. But remember, just because your Ex has not used the exact words quoted does not mean he isn't employing some of the same tactics. It would be impossible to list all the different ways an Ex may express himself. You will need to read between the lines to see if there are similarities between the quotes included here and what your Ex has said to you.

Again, even if you have not seen or experienced a particular trap described in the book, don't just skip ahead. Read each one carefully, because there is a chance that your Ex may use it in the future. The best position for you to be in is to know what he is up to from the very start.

I have worked with many women who have successfully used the tactics outlined in this book to stay away from destructive or dangerous Exes. I have every confidence that they will work for you, too. Good luck, and know that I will be cheering you on from the sidelines.

PART I

Your Ex's Playbook

X

1

Getting to Know His Playbook

Don't fool yourself. Your Ex intends to get you back or get back at you. Maybe both. And make no mistake: He is going to be very strategic about it. You have to be smart, or you will end up playing by his rules instead of doing what is best for you. You have been punished and pushed around long enough. It is time for you to call the shots for yourself. I am not trying to scare you, but to do this you must understand what you are up against.

Your Ex will employ tricks that are time-worn favorites for people who are wired the way he is, and some that he will devise just for you. Both types of sabotage can strike a fatal blow against your ability to stay gone. But there are defenses for almost every ploy, fake out, manipulation, or mind game your Ex uses. By reading about and understanding these plays ahead of time, as well as being familiar with defensive strategies of your own, you will avoid being surprised or unprepared when your former Mr. Wonderful makes a move. Believe me, he will be astonished to see how things have changed—how *you* have changed—when his old and new tricks don't work anymore.

Self-Discovery Exercise #1:
Assessing Your Areas of Vulnerability

First, we should start by getting to know you, because your Ex knows you very well, and we at least need to be on equal footing with him. The Self-Discovery Exercise below will reveal important information about yourself, including where you will likely have the most difficult time resisting your partner's attempts to get you back. It will also identify those areas where you are *less* likely to feel a tug to return. Don't take a long time thinking about your answers to these questions; just go with what your gut tells you. Circle the answer that you believe most applies to you today.

How tempted might you be to return to your Ex if he:

1. Called you over and over and left sad messages begging you to take him back? ("We Need to Talk," page 17)

   • **very**   • **somewhat**   • **not at all**

2. Promised you that he has changed and that things will be different this time? ("I Can Change," page 21)

   • **very**   • **somewhat**   • **not at all**

3. Said that because of all the history you have together, you should give it another shot? ("Don't Throw It All Away," page 32)

   • **very**   • **somewhat**   • **not at all**

4. Told you that he has finally seen the light, and he knows he wants to be with you forever? ("I Can't Live Without You," page 35)

   • **very**   • **somewhat**   • **not at all**

5. Told you all the things you've wanted to hear from him all along? ("I Can Give You What You Need," page 38)

   • **very**   • **somewhat**   • **not at all**

6. Gave you thoughtful compliments about things he used to criticize you for, or things you feel insecure about? ("This Is Your Fault," page 41)

   • **very**   • **somewhat**   • **not at all**

7. Told you that he was going through a tough time, but now he knows how to do better? ("It's Not My Fault," page 48)
   • very   • somewhat   • not at all

8. Told you he is now completely committed to making your dreams of a family or relationship come true? ("I Know All Your Secrets," page 58)
   • very   • somewhat   • not at all

9. Begged you to be his friend? ("I Just Want to Be Friends," page 63)
   • very   • somewhat   • not at all

10. Pleaded with you to think about the kids and how much he loves them? ("What About the Children?" page 67)
    • very   • somewhat   • not at all

11. Made it hard for you to stay away by threatening you or making you afraid? ("You're Going to Be Sorry," page 72)
    • very   • somewhat   • not at all

If you circled "very" or "somewhat" for any of the scenarios, pay extra attention to the page number that is listed at the end of the question. Reading the applicable sections will help you get stronger emotionally in the areas you identified. For now, please know *it is okay that you have these vulnerabilities.* Every woman has areas where she has more or less work to do to stay away from the temptations her Ex may put before her. The important thing is that you have identified what those weaknesses are for you, and now you can focus on learning how to protect yourself if they are used against you. You may not realize it yet, but this is a giant step forward. As you read Chapters 2 and 3 you will see how your Ex may intentionally build his strategy to get you back based on the very weaknesses you just identified. He is no dummy. He knows where you may be most susceptible to his tricks and traps. But with the help of this book you will come to know more about yourself and be able to use this knowledge to stay one step ahead of any trouble he sends your way.

Memory: Your Go-To Player

The period after a breakup almost perfectly reflects the relationship itself. By this I mean that both partners will use the same patterns, behaviors, and coping methods after the relationship is over that they used when they were together.

If, during your relationship, your partner was cold, didn't listen, failed to appreciate your feelings, or was selfish or tenacious about getting his way, then once you've left you can expect him to act the same way. He will still disregard your emotions, minimize your refusal to be with him, think only of himself, and be incredibly persistent about what he wants. Likewise, if in the relationship you were the glue, the peacemaker, or the one who took responsibility for the majority of the problems, after the breakup you may have to fight your urges to resort to those behaviors. All of us have a comfort zone in relationships, and if your comfort zone involves appeasing your partner, you are going to have to fight against your impulses to continue doing so once you've ended things. What is required now is for you to have awareness of your Ex's anger, sadness, accusations, and manipulations without caving in to him or feeling responsible for making him feel better.

Even with the knowledge that people usually act the same way after a relationship ends as they did during the relationship, you may still have some very legitimate fears about what exactly your Ex will do next. The most important tool you have to predict what your Ex will do to get you back is your memory. You have likely separated from, attempted to leave, and/or left your Ex in the past. Or at the very least you've let him know you were considering those options. What did he do when you told him you were thinking this way, or after you acted to separate or leave? Think deeply about this question. He may have had an immediate reaction of anger, sadness, or disbelief. But what did he do in the days, weeks, and months afterward, when he believed you were seriously considering leaving or after you had left? At that point he probably shifted his behavior from its usual patterns, at least temporarily, and acted in ways that were out of the ordinary for him and for the relationship. What were they? Did he become more kind to you? Buy you something? Try to get some romance going? Do things that you had requested of him in the past? Call you more often? Get more angry and demanding? Make you afraid in any way about staying gone? Cry to you? Offer to go to counseling?

Self-Discovery Exercise #2:
Don't Forget What You Remember

Make a list of any unusual or out-of-the-ordinary behaviors you witnessed from your Ex after a past separation, breakup, or conversation you started about these possibilities:

1. _____

2. _____

3. _____

4. _____

5. _____

6. _____

The reason remembering is so important is because whatever he did in the past he is very likely to do again—especially if he thought it worked to get you back. Pay special attention to the sections in this book that relate to the tricks your Ex has used in the past and the X-ing strategies you can employ against them.

Two Crucial Points

Here are two more points to commit to memory as you continue reading:

Crucial Point #1: If you resist going back to your partner one thousand times, and on the one thousand and first time you relent, all your hard work can be unraveled. That doesn't seem fair, but it's the way it is. So when you leave, go with everything you've got (and I don't just mean your cat and toothbrush). Get all of the information and support you can to help yourself be successful. Reading this book can be a part of your commitment to doing everything in your power to succeed.

Crucial Point #2: It is important to know that leaving a bad relationship and not going back are two different things and require different skills. Leaving takes decisiveness, courage, and ultimately bold action. On the other hand, staying gone is not a sprint, it is a marathon. It requires determination, commitment, vigilance, and lots and lots of endurance. Some people are good at the leaving but tend to lose their resolve over time, and some are good at staying gone but struggle to initially sever the relationship. *You must do both successfully in order to get on with your life, attain peace of mind, and secure the possibility of a happier future.* In the following chapters, like a good coach, I will help you prepare for the marathon ahead by showing you how to build your strength, stay focused on your goal, and soar over the obstacles your Ex will create to trip you up.

2 Your Ex's Defensive Plays

I've got to hand it to manipulative Exes: When it comes to dreaming up ways to get their partners back, they are so darn talented! There seems to be no end to the creativity, subtlety, and cunning that some men will use against their unsuspecting former partners. For me, seeing Exes behave this way is similar to watching footage of a bomb explosion. I am at once amazed by the bomb's power and the ingenuity that went into creating it, yet terrified by the destruction and harm it causes.

Despite the seemingly infinite number of ploys I have seen Exes dream up over the years, all of them fit into two categories. The first is defensive plays, and that's what this chapter is about. The second is offensive plays, described in the next chapter.

Defensive plays are those things an Ex does to defend against your completely giving up on him or the relationship. They help him keep his foot in the door with you, and they create a lingering emotional connection between you and him. These tactics tend to be sneaky and subtle and often come disguised as flattery, apologies, gifts, or promises. However they are packaged, your Ex's defensive plays will create a real and ongoing temptation for you to turn your well-intentioned breakup into a thing of the past.

As I suggested in the Introduction, even if some of these scenarios don't seem to apply to your situation, please don't skip ahead. Read them all. If your Ex hasn't used some of them yet, he may do so eventually.

"We Need to Talk"

Most Exes will try to contact you. And when I say they will try to contact you, I mean they will make it their full-time job/ meaning for existence/highest goal in life to get you to listen to them.

To accomplish this they will use the phone, computer, letters, mutual friends and acquaintances, smoke signals, skywriting, and any other form of communication they can think of. They do this because, just like in court, you can't sway the judge and jury unless you get to present your case. (There are some lawyers who could learn a thing or two from certain Exes about how to creatively present the facts.) Your Ex may or may not already have tried to contact you. Either way, it will help if you know why he is intent on doing so.

The number-one reason why he is trying to call you is because it is dramatically easier for you to heal and move on from him if you are *not* still talking to him. Your Ex knows that unless he can open up a dialogue with you, the chances of your going back to him are much slimmer. Without communication, a number of his strategies to get you back are much more difficult. See the list that follows for some of his reasons for wanting to stay in touch with you.

Reasons Why Your Ex Wants to Communicate with You

- to keep tabs on you
- to encourage you to feel guilty
- to help you remember the good times
- to be cute, charming, and funny
- to make promises to change
- to make you think your decisions are wrong or unfair
- to make a threat or badger you into coming back
- to give his opinion about how you spend your time, who you see, where you go, what you wear, what you eat, what you believe, etc.
- to show you how committed he now is to the relationship
- to apologize and beg
- to trick himself into thinking he is still having a relationship with you
- to use your secrets against you or otherwise manipulate you
- to tell you how much you are hurting him
- to lie or try to erase the truth
- to rationalize what he did to you
- to move things one step further by getting you to meet him, go on just one date, give him one more chance, etc.

That list contains a lot of twisted reasons for trying to contact someone. Now you can see why he is dead serious about getting through to you. *Without communication, almost all of the weapons he will use to get you back are disarmed.* That is why he will commit many resources, including time and money, to this battle. And it really is a battle to get your attention, destroy your peace of mind, and weaken your resolve. Think about it. The more times you talk to him, the more opportunities he will have to say just the right thing or combination of things to get you back.

All of us have a weakness, and if he pinpoints yours correctly it shouldn't take too long before he has you second-guessing your decision to leave. Will it be ten conversations, twenty conversations, or just one before he twists your logic around? It is hard to tell. But why risk it?

Every time you talk to him you are playing Russian roulette with your future. And every time he reaches you he is motivated to do it again because he is more certain that you are willing to negotiate your decision. If you don't want to go back, why would you send this message or any message? It is like the game Battleship. You get chance after chance to guess where your enemy's ships are hiding. There are only so many places on the game board to position the ships, and if your opponent gets enough tries to sink your battleship, eventually you lose. Don't let your Ex sink your ship because you gave him too many guesses at what would work to get you back.

Another reason not to talk to your Ex is because doing so uses up your vital emotional energy. Whether it is defending yourself, explaining for the tenth time why you left, fending off accusations, or deflecting his charm and compliments, all these maneuvers take mental and emotional energy you cannot spare.

A final downside to talking to your Ex is that he may be pretty darn good at playing word games or twisting what you say to mean other things. This can be very confusing and entangle you in his side of the story. Save yourself a lot of grief by cutting off communication and meaning it.

Technology Tip

Don't forget about how technology may factor into your Ex's attempts to maintain contact with you. If you use e-mail, Facebook, Foursquare, or dating websites; if you have a blog; if you belong to chat groups or online communities; or if you use any other type of social media; your Ex may utilize any of them to try to intercept you and get you talking to him. Don't be fooled into thinking that communicating by computer creates a safe distance between you and your Ex. You may not be face to face with him, but interacting screen to screen can be just as dangerous.

Strategies for cutting off his ability to get information about or communicate with you online include: changing any passwords or usernames he may know, especially for your e-mail; blocking his access to sites such as Facebook, LinkedIn, and Twitter, or making your participation on those sites private; changing your screen names or discontinuing your participation in chat groups or online communities he knows you visit.

Look for other Technology Tips throughout this book for more information on how to protect yourself and your use of digital technology. A great organization with even more information on this subject is the National Network to End Domestic Violence. Their contact information is listed in the Resources section, located at the end of the book.

Remember, if you are making the transition away from an Ex, you may need to consider how secure or private a site is before you participate as a user. If there's any chance that your information could be acquired and used inappropriately by your Ex, think carefully before you log in.

Recommended X-ing Strategies

Fear not. There are countermeasures for every weapon in your Ex's arsenal. Located at the end of each section in Chapters 2 and 3 are three Recommended X-ing Strategies that can help you neutralize the ploy described in that section. Because every situation is different, *please use your judgment about which of these X-ing Strategies will work best for you.* There are even more time-tested strategies for you to choose from in Chapters 4 and 5. Taken together, all of these tactics will make staying away from your Ex much, much easier.

1. Use a Freedom Journal (p. 87)
2. Mum's the Word (p. 95)
3. Shut Down Friends with Messages (p. 98)

"I Can Change"

This ever-so-common ploy of Exes the world over takes the form of one of the following lies:

1. "I will change."
2. "You can change me."
3. "I will get help and others will change me."
4. "God will change me."
5. "You can change and that will change me."

Take a good look at them, ladies. Five short, seemingly innocent sentences. Looks can be deceiving. Every single one of these promises is packed with the potential to send you straight back to your Ex. These lies are as old as time itself and have wreaked havoc on the lives of hundreds of thousands of smart, big-hearted, beautiful women.

I imagine that from the beginning of humanity, cavemen who acted like jerks to cavewomen hid behind statements like these. And those unlucky cavewomen had to learn a lesson that unfortunately women today still have to learn: It is not what your partner *says* he will do; it is what he actually *does* that counts. This is because the only real predictor of what someone will do in the future is what they have done in the past.

These lies worked ages ago, and they work now. *Most hurtful Exes will use at least one of them to tempt you back into the relationship. Some really crafty Exes may use more than one.*

It is important to point out that at the time he says it, your Ex may or may not know he is telling a lie. Many Exes believe they can and will change, either on their own or through the help of others. But changing is simply not that easy. Your Ex has developed a huge number of habits, thinking patterns, and beliefs over the course of a lifetime, and these have all gone into shaping his behaviors toward you. He may be consciously aware of them, or he may not be. To make meaningful change he would need to seriously commit himself to figuring all this out. And that takes lots of time and effort. Sadly, from my experience working with women, *it is very rare that this occurs.* Don't let yourself be fooled by a bunch of empty promises.

Let's review each of these lies a little more carefully.

▶ Lie #1: "I Will Change"

Sorry if I sound pessimistic, but the chance that someone will actually change from not being good to you to being good to you is incredibly remote. Usually what happens is that someone can change for a few weeks or months, but eventually they return to who they are. And who they are is someone who is unable to consistently give you what you need. Asking you to come back by promising that he'll change is basically like asking you to buy a lottery ticket whose odds are a million to one. Sure, you have a chance of winning, but 999,999 of the people who take the gamble will lose. And what do they lose, you might ask? They lose the opportunity to make a better future for themselves. And that is a hell of a gamble to make. If your Ex has made this promise before and failed to stick to it, his proposition is more like asking you to stake your future on winning a lottery that you don't even have a ticket for.

I know that this practical view of people can be hard to keep in mind when your deepest feelings are involved, and that it is generally seen as supportive and loving when you hope that someone can do better than they have done before. But if you have to put yourself into a deep state of denial to be with someone, it's time to try a different approach. It is like the old saying: "Fool me once, shame on you. Fool me twice, shame on me."

Variations on "I Will Change"

Here is what this lie may sound like coming from your Ex:

- "I was an idiot before. Just give me a chance. I will be better to you this time."
- "You can trust me. I've stopped drinking."
- "I know I hurt you. I will stop being so controlling."
- "I'll treat you the way you deserve."
- "I will listen to what you need this time, and we will work it out."
- "You know I can do better if you will just hang in there with me."
- "You'll see, I will not lose my temper like that anymore."
- "I will spend more time with you and the kids."
- "I will be more supportive of you."
- "You were right, I was the one who needed to change."

▶ Lie #2: "You Can Change Me"

Oh, this is a good one! It is basically an offer for you to become his counselor, mother, priest, and conscience all rolled into one. This lie can be particularly attractive to those of us who want to help others, especially the people we love who show so much potential. It can be very gratifying and a boost to our ego to think that our Ex would essentially trust us to oversee his rehabilitation. It can also make us feel like we are getting back some of the power and respect we deserve. After all, he is saying that he will now let us run the show and tell him what he needs to do. And, honestly, we may know or have some pretty good ideas about what our Ex needs to do to get his life together and become a better partner. Here are the problems though:

1. Most Exes don't want to change; they just want to get you back, and this is one way to do it.

2. You can know what your Ex needs, but if your Ex isn't committed to the change, it doesn't matter. And if your Ex *were* committed to the change, he likely would have sought the answer on his own, found it, and pursued it.

3. Even if your Ex is committed to following through on your recommendations, it can be a long time, if ever, before you see any change. Is it really worth the risk, the years of pain while waiting to see results, and the sizable chance that those changes will never come?

4. It is likely that if change isn't achieved, *you* will feel like a failure. You may even feel responsible for sticking around to make things right. This is the opposite of how it should be, but I have seen it too many times to doubt it. I have witnessed many giving, committed, and selfless women fruitlessly try to manage their partners' emotions, use of alcohol or drugs, employment, relationships with others, or behavior. Often these women

end up feeling as though they didn't help enough, do enough, encourage him enough, make the right suggestions, or be what he really needed. They end up staying in the relationship in an attempt to find the perfect formula to help him change. Despite all this effort, they are essentially wasting what they have to give the world. This is a terrible and impossible trap.

When you start measuring your worth by how much you have changed someone else, you are in trouble. Think about it. How many hours, days, or years have you spent attempting to change other people? For most of us, if we are completely honest, the answer to this question can be sickening. So much time, energy, and emotion—all down the drain with nothing to show for it.

Do not let your Ex win you over with the lie that you can help him change. He may try. Be on alert for promises like "Just tell me what to do. I will do anything you say to get you back." Or, "I know you are the only one who can help me." Or, "Without your help I won't make it." If you hear statements like these—which make *you* responsible for *his* change—pull the emergency break.

▶ Lie #3: "I Will Get Help and Others Will Change Me"

Experts. We have been trained since childhood to depend on them, be they doctors, mechanics, counselors, attorneys, or teachers. We put our faith in experts and trust that they can help us with everything from getting our cars moving to getting our bodies working. Most of the time experts perform valuable services that we cannot do for ourselves. Many times when women find themselves in a bad relationship they think, "I can't get this guy to shape up, but maybe an expert can." Then they try, usually unsuccessfully, to get their partner to see an expert for help so they can find some relief from his bad behaviors.

The five types of experts women most commonly encourage their partners to see are:

1. a counselor or therapist for individual, couples, or family counseling
2. a psychiatrist
3. a substance abuse counselor, or an Alcoholics Anonymous, Narcotics Anonymous, or Sex Addicts Anonymous sponsor and/or group
4. someone who provides spiritual guidance
5. teachers, healers, and assorted community leaders and professionals

The good news is that all of these people really do have the potential to help. I believe so much in people's ability to help each other by sharing their expertise that I have written this book about a topic on which I consider myself an expert. But as much as I believe in professionals' abilities to make things better, the somewhat bad news is that their effectiveness depends on the client's cooperation and full participation. A doctor's diagnosis is not of much help if the patient doesn't take his or her medication, and my book wouldn't do you much good if you just left it on the shelf. Similarly, just because a person goes to the best counselor, most effective faith leader, or most caring sponsor in no way means that he will succeed in becoming a better partner.

This is something that your Ex hopes you will forget when he uses Lie #3—when he tells you that he can get help and miraculously be changed.

How does this lie work? It's pretty simple.

Step 1: Your Ex comes up with an expert that he believes you think will help him. Or he finally says that he will go to an expert you have urged him to see before.

Step 2: He tells you about his plan to see the professional, usually before going to a session. He might say, "You know, I have been thinking about it, and you are right. We should go to couples counseling." Or, "I do have a problem with alcohol. I will get sober by going to those AA meetings you told me about." Or, "I will go to a counselor so I can work out what happened to me as a child. Then I will be able to control my temper better."

Step 3: After making these statements, he expects you to reward him with your return, or at least to be open to negotiating the idea of coming back. He also expects you to be thrilled, grateful, supportive, and his biggest cheerleader.

Step 4: Once he has secured your affection again, he quietly abandons his efforts to actually get the help he once claimed he was so eager to receive.

In the moment when he tells you he is going to seek help, you may be incredibly relieved and happy for him. You may feel vindicated, because you've probably been encouraging him to get help for a long time. But don't let that relief or sense of being proven right overwhelm your good sense. As we talked about, going to a professional does not by itself assure successful change. It's like they say, "It is all just corn until it pops." In this case, it is all just words until they are acted on. And frankly, it is the rare Ex who both goes to the professional (many say they will but never do) *and* shows the motivation, dedication, and perseverance required to do the work necessary to make a difference in himself.

So just because he says he is going to get help, do not jump to the conclusion that things will be different. There are many, many steps in between. In fact, if the underlying reason why your Ex is saying he will get help is because he is trying to get you back, it is almost certain that he will not do what it takes to actually change. *Instead, he will only do enough to get you back.* Once you are back he might continue to get help for a short time just to prevent you from catching on and leaving again, but he will never be genuinely invested, and therefore will never get the result you are hoping for. *This highlights something that is true for many women: You, not your Ex, are probably the one who is much more willing to go through the often painful process required to bring about real personal transformation.* For many a manipulative Ex, seeing a professional, or saying that he will, is just another tactic he can use to get you to ignore your good judgment and let an irrational hope get the best of you.

▶ Lie #4: "God Will Change Me"

It is disturbing to think that someone would use his belief in God, or perhaps *your* belief in God, as a tool to get you back. A part of me wishes I'd just dreamed up this scenario. But, alas, it has not all been a bad dream. I have seen many cases in which an Ex claimed that he was going to use his faith to change his behavior toward a partner. And because most of us want to believe that our faith can transform us, and because faith truly can have this power, a woman usually feels like a real jerk when she second-guesses someone who makes this claim. Unfortunately, this can play into your Ex's hands. If you cannot doubt the truth of a promise for fear of being too cynical, then you just have to rely on what he tells you. This is not a good position to be in with your Ex.

To be fair, sometimes your Ex may really think that improving his spiritual life will stop his bad behavior. Other times, an Ex has no intention of doing what he says, or he doesn't believe it will work. He is just saying what he feels he must say to get you back.

Here is the hard truth. In my experience helping women—whether a woman is dealing with an Ex who is genuinely seeking spiritual help for his problems, or with an Ex who is just using this lie as another tactic—the chances of his making real change on the strength of this promise are not good. Of course, there are dramatic stories of people who find their spirituality and turn their whole life around. Those tales are wonderful and inspiring. But those individuals are rare. That is what makes them such great stories.

Dramatically more common is for an Ex to make a half-hearted attempt to do some reading of his sacred text, or go to church a few times, and then run out of motivation to continue. This pattern happens even more frequently when his partner returns to him, because much of his original motivation—to encourage his partner's return—is gone. *One has to wonder, if he knew that getting in touch with his spirituality might help him be more kind, why didn't he do it before he made you so unhappy you had to leave?*

If you have strong spiritual beliefs, or if you have had a transformative experience with religion, it can be incredibly tempting to feel that an increased closeness with a higher power is the answer for your Ex, too. It can be difficult to separate your own experience with religion from that of your Ex. But this is what you must do in order to discern if your Ex is using religion as a tool to get you back. We have all known people who attend a religious service one day and the next day are up to no good. Just because someone goes through the motions of, say, reading the Quran, Bible, or Torah, or contributing to their faith community, does not prevent them from going home and repeating their shameful behaviors. Don't be confused by someone who is saying the right words and even doing some of the right things, but who will ultimately cause you the same pain.

▶ Lie #5: "You Can Change and That Will Change Me"

I saved the best lie for last. This one is a classic for Exes who can't seem to take responsibility for anything they do. Any form of Lie #5 should send you running. It is a very bad omen for what is ahead if you get back together. It removes the responsibility for his changing from him and puts it on you. It makes *you* responsible for how he feels and for what he does as a result of those feelings. It encourages you to think, "I can do better, and then he will do better, and then we will be happy." But the terrible thing about this lie is that his temper, lack of affection, coldness, jealousy, mood swings, or controlling ways are not and were never about you.

Here is an important truth that I have observed over and over: *People tend to be the same no matter who they're in a relationship with.* I know this is hard to believe, and he may have told you just the opposite. Of course, some people can bring out better or worse sides of you, but for most of us there is a consistency between who we are, for better or worse, from one relationship to the next. A person who blames, disrespects, or belittles their partner has probably repeated this behavior in every romantic relationship they've been in since puberty and will do so until their last relationship—no matter who they date or marry. So don't take blame that isn't yours.

We all have imperfections that we would like to change. But if your partner points at a weakness of yours and says it is the reason why he treated you badly, he is just trying to hide the truth. Your partner treated you badly because he chose to. Plain and simple. We don't make each other do things. And just as you did not make him do the bad things he did, you cannot somehow now make him do the good things you want him to do. It is entirely up to him. If he is putting this weight on you, it is a great indicator that he doesn't accept responsibility for his actions and therefore will never be able to change them.

Examples of "You Can Change and That Will Change Me"

Here is what this lie might sound like coming from your Ex:

- "If you didn't [insert thing he doesn't like here], I wouldn't lose my temper."
- "If you would just do what I told you to, we wouldn't argue."
- "If you weren't so stubborn, we would get along fine."
- "If you didn't start the arguments, we wouldn't have them."
- "You're the one who [insert bad thing here], not me!"
- "If you ever fixed yourself up, I wouldn't look at other women."
- "If you would just listen to what I am saying, I wouldn't have to raise my voice."
- "If you gave me more attention, I wouldn't be so jealous."
- "If you didn't drive me crazy with all your nagging, I would give you what you want."
- "If you didn't hang out with those friends so much, we wouldn't fight so much."
- "If you would just let yourself be happy, you would see that everything is fine."
- "If you would just look at what you did to hurt us, we could be better."

I think you get the idea. Basically, your Ex is letting you know it is all your fault that things are screwed up. Hopefully, after reading this, you will realize that it is his perception of the facts that are screwed up—not you.

"Don't Throw It All Away"

The good investor knows when to buy. The great investor knows when to buy *and* when to sell. If you hold on to a bad investment too long, or keep pouring money and time into a project that is doomed, you can lose everything. It's the same with relationships. With some relationships and some people, no matter how much time, energy, or good intention you put into them, they are not going to get better. And it is not your fault. What is your "fault" is if you refuse to see the writing on the wall and deal with the facts.

One way of knowing whether you are dealing with the facts or just dreaming about what could be is by understanding the difference between possibility and probability. Is it possible to reunite with your Ex and for things to magically get better? Yes. Is it probable? No. Similarly, is it possible that when I go to the coffee shop that sells my favorite chocolate milkshakes I won't order one? Yes. Is it probable? Hell, no! And I know this, so unless I want to drink a chocolate milkshake (which I often do), I don't go to that coffee shop.

Bottom line: If you don't want the same relationship you had, don't get back together with the Ex you had it with. The difference between possible and probable is very important. If you are pinning all your hopes on the *possibility* of your partner changing, you will likely wait forever.

It can seem wrong to view relationships in this matter-of-fact way. In most areas of our lives—whether it is a job, an education, or a hobby—if we try hard and put time in, eventually we get results. Why wouldn't the attempted improvement of a partner be the same?

Because you are dealing with another person.

When you were together with your Ex, you most likely tried all kinds of things to help him see the light and change his behavior. Having talked to over a thousand women who have tried every method to change their partners, I am convinced that if the time, creativity, and brilliance they put into transforming their doomed relationships were channeled into space exploration, we would have populated Mars by now. Women are truly amazing in this way. One thing is for sure, we do not give up easily. Sometimes this is a really good thing, but other times... not so much.

A lot of us pride ourselves on our dedication to the ones we love. And this is good. But at some point it can be a liability. Like Kenny Rogers sang in the song "The Gambler," "You got to know when to hold 'em, know when to fold 'em, know when to walk away, and know when to run." That running part can be so darned difficult. Even the most screwed-up, lying, cheating jerk on the planet probably has an ex-girlfriend or ex-wife who still wonders if she couldn't have turned him around. And the answer simply is no. He was never going to change. Not for her, not for you, not for anyone. The only question was how much of her life, energy, and goodness he was going to take. This may be the same question you are facing.

One client I worked with was an older, very talented, successful artist. Unlike you, she hadn't yet left her partner. I asked her why she stayed with her husband, who for a long time had been emotionally unavailable and extremely critical. He had recently pushed her off the bed in anger. She said, "I put twenty years into this marriage. I can't just walk away."

The fact that she had made such a huge investment prevented her from seeing that all her efforts were in vain, and that there was no point at which they would start to pay off. She could stay committed to her spouse forever, and things might actually get worse! The reality of relationships can be very cruel. And many, many amazing, smart women have wasted huge amounts of their lives trying to leave an unhealthy relationship only to have their partners drag them back in. If you recognize when your Ex is trying to tempt you into wasting more time on him, you don't have to be one of those women.

Here is the creepy part. Your Ex knows that you have tried long and hard to make things work and that throughout the relationship you really believed things could be better. He can play on those old hopes and dreams by reminding you of how much "fun" that was. See the list that follows.

Reminders of Your Investment in the Relationship

After a breakup he might say to you:

- "Come on, we have ten years together!"
- "You're not just going to throw it all away, are you?"
- "Our love is stronger than this."
- "Remember how good things were in the beginning?"
- "I will listen to you this time."
- "No one will ever know you the way I do."
- "We have history together."

All of these statements are intended to get you to put your relationship-fixer hat back on and to recommit to doing the impossible: changing your Ex. And the implied reason why you should do that is either because you have already been doing it for so long or because this time things will be different.

This tactic works more often than you might imagine. We can get so wrapped up in what we have already given that we are blinded to how much more they can take. And believe me, bad Exes can take it all.

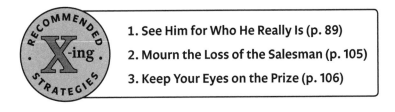

1. See Him for Who He Really Is (p. 89)
2. Mourn the Loss of the Salesman (p. 105)
3. Keep Your Eyes on the Prize (p. 106)

"I Can't Live Without You"

This defensive strategy of your Ex's can be tricky to detect. He knows that you've been hurt and frustrated by his lack of appreciation for you and for the relationship, so now he changes his tune. His aim is to convince you that he has finally realized what a good thing he had in you, that he has seen the light, that he has had an "aha" moment.

▶ "Aha" Moments

An "aha" moment is the instant when the light bulb over your head switches on and you suddenly get it, whatever "it" is. It occurs after you've wrestled with something for a long time— say, a relationship issue, a big question about yourself, or a problem at work that you've been trying to figure out. The moment when you finally have the answer you have been seeking and you know what direction to take is an "aha" moment. You probably had an "aha" moment when you decided you had to leave your Ex, when all the evidence came together. The thing that triggered this awareness may have been something small but degrading (the millionth time he expected you to do his dishes) or something big and shocking (he hit you). Whatever it is that sparks your "aha" moment, this flash of clarity has the power to lead to a significant change.

Exes often report that they had an "aha" moment after their partners left. Sometimes they genuinely think they've had one, and other times they just think it sounds convincing. Either way, an Ex will try hard to communicate to a woman that her leaving has prompted a tidal shift in his thinking. If your Ex uses this method to get you back, here is what he might say:

Favorite "Aha" Moments of Exes

- "I have learned my lesson and I want you back."
- "I see now how much I need you."
- "I never thought I could miss someone so much."
- "Your leaving me was just what I needed to see that I can't live without you."
- "I am ready for us to have a baby/get married."
- "I now know that you are the woman I want to spend the rest of my life with."
- "This breakup gave me the time and space to see that you are truly the only woman for me."
- "I didn't see how much you do for me until you weren't there."
- "Your leaving broke me out of my commitment phobia. I can't live without you."
- "I see now that what we had was good. We just have some problems to work out."

These statements are some of the most popular ones used by Exes, but there are certainly others. What they have in common is the intent to convince you that he is somehow a new man.

▶ "Oh Crap" Moments

Unfortunately, what is far more likely than his having experienced an "aha" moment is that your Ex experienced a strong "oh crap" moment. "Oh crap! Who is going to cook dinner/do the laundry/take care of the kids/pay the bills/be there for me?" "Oh crap! I never actually thought she would leave." "Oh crap! How am I going to get her back?" "Oh crap! She is really pissed this time."

The "oh crap" moment is different from a genuine "aha" moment in that it comes from the selfish part of your Ex that *liked* the way things were and is afraid of the way things will be now that you have left. *It does not lead to a change.* It may lead your Ex to act very kindly to you for a while, but that is because he wants things to be the way they were. If I am not mistaken, you dislike the way things were. That is why you left.

Your Ex has gotten used to the perks you provided to him. Whether it was regular sex, help cleaning the house, cooking, caring for the children, maintaining relationships with family and friends, a convenient outlet for his anger or stress, help with paying the bills, or even avoiding loneliness, there are lots of reasons why your Ex wishes you hadn't left him that have nothing to do with his love for you. He is thinking "Oh crap!" because he is either going to have to get off his butt and work hard to get you back, go through the trouble of recruiting and training a replacement for you, or take on the additional responsibilities you used to fill. Just because your Ex has an "oh crap" moment does not mean he is a different person or that things would be any different if you went back. But since your Ex wants you to think he is a new man, he masks his "oh crap" moment as an "aha" moment. After all, you would never go back because he said, "Look baby, I really don't have time to take care of the house, the dog, the kids, or to send my mother a card at Christmas, so I am willing to overlook your dumping me if you will get your butt back here and get to work."

OR

"I know I have a crazy temper and take the people I am with for granted. I am afraid if you leave me I will never find anyone else as good as you to put up with my crap, so let's just forget this breakup and get back together."

OR

"I know I don't respect you the way I should and that I treat you badly, but that works great for me. Don't you want me back?"

There is a reason why you don't encounter phrases like these in romance novels or Hallmark cards. But this is what you might hear if your Ex were honest or truly in touch with his motivations for wanting you back.

You don't have to be fooled by the way he disguises his "oh crap" moment, and you don't have to feel sorry for him. He should have lots of "oh crap" moments, because he messed up a really good thing.

1. Cut Off Communication (p. 79)

2. See Him for Who He Really Is (p. 89)

3. Put Your Happiness First (p. 107)

"I Can Give You What You Need"

What is the one thing you wish your Ex had done when you were together? You should really think about this question, because chances are your Ex knows the answer.

Do you wish he had told you that you are beautiful, asked how your day was, listened to you more, been a better parent, shared his feelings, or showed you more affection? All of these unmet needs are vulnerable areas that your Ex will exploit to try to get you back. Using them against you is an obvious and effective maneuver to resuscitate the relationship.

You have probably communicated these wants and desires to your Ex many times, and many times he has not delivered. But now that you are gone he suddenly remembers to send you flowers, tells you all the sweet words you had been waiting to hear, or tries to get you into bed by making a big romantic gesture. Now he seems willing to be the man you always wanted. Possibly the man you fell in love with. How can you know if he will stay this way or if it is just a trick?

One thing that may make this question even harder to answer is that it can feel great to finally get the attention and recognition you have been craving. It is similar to sitting down to your first meal after a fast, or finally having dinner after skipping breakfast and lunch. Everything tastes awesome. You never knew you liked Brussels sprouts so much or that dry toast could taste like cake. If you hadn't been so hungry you probably wouldn't be going gaga over your dinner. The same goes for our emotional "stomachs." If we haven't been nourished emotionally for a long time, getting a few morsels of care and affection can be incredibly satisfying and can make us incredibly hungry for more.

The truth is that if your partner had been fulfilling your needs all along, you wouldn't be so darned grateful for crumbs, but right now your emptiness will definitely work against you. This is why there is usually a window of time after a breakup during which if the Ex does enough groveling, promising, gift giving, and making up for what he has done wrong, he can usually win back his partner. The problem is that even though your Ex may be very willing right now to put in the time and effort it takes to make you happy, once you return his motivation will dry up.

One woman I worked with had a rust-bucket of a car. She lived in a rural area and had always wanted a truck. After she left her Ex, he bought her a brand new truck in her favorite color, green. She was so overwhelmed with gratitude that she went back to him. A few months later she and her partner were fighting again. One day when she tried to go to work, the truck would not start. Her partner had removed the truck's starter and had left her at their house in the country with no transportation. This story illustrates that what your Ex gives you today, he can take away tomorrow.

1. Cut Off Communication (p. 79)

2. Test His Words (p. 86)

3. Use a Freedom Journal (p. 87)

3 *Your Ex's Offensive Plays*

Defensive plays encompass half of the strategies that your Ex may use to get you back. Offensive plays are the other half. Just like offensive plays in football, the ones your Ex uses are designed to gain him additional ground at your expense. But instead of yardage on the field, it is emotional territory—your self-esteem, peace of mind, and hopes for a better future—that he is trying to steal. And once he shifts from playing defensively to playing offensively, he won't be nice about it. Rather, he will rely on the time-tested tactics of blame, shame, manipulation, deceit, guilt, and fear.

I'd like to think, as I am sure you would, that someone who once professed to love you would never use these awful weapons against you. But I have seen it happen too many times, to too many good women, to doubt it. I only hope that you will be alert to the possibility that your Ex may be willing to stoop so low and will be ready if he does.

"This Is Your Fault"

Throughout your relationship, your Ex probably brought up issues he had with you. Maybe he didn't like a part of your personality, the way you live your life, how you treated him, or the way you look.

▶ Digging the Hole

By communicating his disapproval, he is "digging the hole": attempting to make you feel bad about yourself. Here's how this might sound coming out of his mouth:

"Dig the Hole" Statements

- "You should be more confident."
- "I hate the way you're always nagging me."
- "Oh, we're eating fast food again."
- "You really should take better care of yourself."
- "You are such a drama queen."
- "Are you really going to wear that?"
- "You know I love you, but you are getting on my nerves/ you talk too much/sometimes you are so stupid."
- "You are so stubborn."
- "You're crazy."
- "You need to chill out."
- "That outfit looks trashy."
- "You should eat healthier."
- "You never listen to me."
- "Why can't you be more like Will's girlfriend? She is so great at _____."
- "Can't you ever just be happy?"
- "You are such a [insert curse word here]."

Take a minute and, as painful as it might be, jot down the "dig the hole" statements your Ex used against you.

Self-Discovery Exercise #3:
What Holes Did Your Ex Dig?

1. _____

2. _____

3. _____

All of these statements don't just evaporate once they've been made. They lodge between our ears and impact what we think about ourselves and our behaviors. The countless women I've talked to who've been in bad relationships—even the ones who have been in physically abusive relationships and have been beaten black and blue—all agree on one thing. It is the things their Ex *said to them* that created the wounds that are hardest to heal.

Even if we physically remove our Exes from our lives we may still hear their voices and criticisms in our heads. In effect, they are never really gone. Their favorite put-downs and disrespectful words still affect us—how we feel about ourselves, how we parent, how we do or don't allow ourselves to embrace freedom and pleasure.

In more serious cases, a woman may lead a life largely controlled by her Ex when he isn't even around anymore! I have talked to women who, for example, say they would like to get a certain job but don't believe they are smart enough or have enough skills to do so. Sometimes a hurtful partner will tell a woman these things outright. More commonly, however, over time he'll make little jabs at her self-esteem. He won't come right out and call her stupid, but he will second-guess her, take opportunities to point out when she screws up, or simply never acknowledge her brilliance, skills, or capabilities. Do not underestimate how your Ex's unspoken words can impact you as much as his verbal criticism or nit-picking. When you don't hear kind words from your partner (e.g., "You are lovable/good/

special/talented"), your brain tends to draw certain conclusions. Bad ones. These women received very clear messages about themselves, with or without being explicitly criticized. And the messages acquired a lot of weight and power in their decision-making about important aspects of their life, like whether to try for a new job.

My client Tyra had been so torn down by her husband's demeaning comments and the environment of contempt he created around her that she stopped knowing what she liked to eat. Tyra, convinced that she was not worthy, had deferred to her husband on almost all decision-making. One of the many subjects on which she gave in to him was what they should eat, and after three decades of marriage she stopped knowing what foods she liked, wanted to eat, or got pleasure from. Tyra's disconnection from something as basic as her own sensory experience of taste gives you an idea of how much a dysfunctional Ex can take from a person. Because Tyra had been repeatedly discouraged by her husband from trusting her own decisions, even a small errand like a trip to the grocery store caused her anxiety and fear. Experimenting to rediscover what she liked to eat and taking time to really taste and find enjoyment in food again was just one of many barriers Tyra had to overcome in order to regain her confidence and stay free from her husband.

Perhaps your Ex chose to pick apart something you considered a strength. Whether it was your high-school diploma or college degree, your pretty hair, your generosity, or the way you made fried chicken—any of them was a potential target, and taking aim at it put him in the driver's seat and made it easier for him to get what he wanted from you.

Or maybe his strategy was to say hurtful things about an area of weakness for you. Maybe you didn't feel great about your weight, your parenting skills, your lovability, or the car you drove. We all have things we don't like about ourselves, and each of them presents an area of vulnerability that a not-so-nice guy could exploit. He might have done this by making fun of you, continually pointing out your struggles, using them as excuses for his bad behavior, or simply never offering the kindness and support that might have comforted you.

It is easy for an Ex to get you where it hurts. You don't need any convincing that this part of you is broken. So when he says or does things that deepen your feelings of inferiority, you may just assume he's telling you the hard truth. If your Ex says, "Your thighs are fat," or, "You should work out more," and you are insecure about your weight, you might think, "I wish he wouldn't say that, but he is right, I really have let myself go." Whether you are pleasantly plump or just think you are is irrelevant, because feeling worse about yourself can make it even harder to create positive change, and each of your failures provides him another opportunity to degrade you. Ugh! This is a bad cycle, and one that can definitely be used against you after you have left the relationship.

The criticisms your Ex has made repeatedly are particularly dangerous. To use a fairly common example, if he told you somewhat regularly that you are too sensitive, take things too seriously, cry too much, or are too emotional, it is likely that you eventually started believing him to some degree. Perhaps this view of yourself wouldn't have occurred to you if your Ex hadn't suggested it. Either way, it can give him an opening. If he can convince you that your sensitivity has caused you to blow things out of proportion or end things too hastily, then you may start second-guessing your decision. In this way, the ideas he has planted in your mind are like landmines to which he controls the detonator. He will try to use your insecurities—over issues real or imagined—to destroy your reasons for leaving him.

▶ Filling the Hole

If this doesn't work, he can "fill the hole," the other part of the equation. If he can't make you feel crappy enough to doubt your decision to leave him, he may flip the script, turn on the charm, and try a little sweet talk instead. After making you worry that you're oversensitive, for example, he could "fill the hole" by validating your feelings, telling you that you were right all along, and apologizing for saying those things. I know it's messed up, but I am telling you this ploy works. After someone has criticized you and you've started to believe them, it feels great to hear the opposite.

Here are some more examples of how an Ex can make you feel bad about yourself and then turn it around on you.

Digging and Filling the Hole

He has made you feel...	Then he says...
Unattractive	"You are so beautiful."
Not good at something	"I really do like your cooking/how you parent/your handling of the finances. I wish I'd told you that more often."
Not smart	"You have always been smarter than I am."
Not loving enough	"If it weren't for you I wouldn't be anything."
Not forgiving enough	"You've given me so many chances that I didn't deserve."
Not fair to him	"You are the one who has kept us together."
Too assertive	"I respect how hard you've had to push to get us here."
Too needy	"I want to be there for you now. I see that I was closed off to you."

Too emotional	"I hate that I've made you cry. It is my fault. I know I didn't treat you right."
Too verbal	"I know I need to learn how to talk things out."
Too hard on him	"I deserve your anger."

More "Fill the Hole" Statements

- "You are the best person I know."
- "I never deserved you."
- "You are the only one who can love me."
- "I can't make it without you."
- "You are my rock."
- "You've always had me figured out."
- "I never appreciated you like I should have."
- "You are the best thing that ever happened to me."
- "You are so sexy."
- "I miss making love to you."
- "I just want you to know how loved you are."
- "I am sorry I told you those things—they aren't true."
- "I want you to be the mother of my children."
- "You are the best mother a kid could ever have."
- "I need you."
- "You make my life so much better."
- "You are so funny."
- "You are the best person I know."
- "I want to make a life with you."
- "You always believed in me."

This dig-the-hole/fill-the-hole tactic is incredibly effective. It can actually make someone feel grateful to the person who hurt them so many times. If someone burns us and then applies a little aloe, the aloe will feel good, but that doesn't take away the fact that we were burned. And, frankly, I would rather not be burned in the first place. By staying away from your Ex you won't get to feel the salve of the soothing words he uses to make things right, but nor will you have to feel the sting of being burned by him yet again.

1. Cut Off Communication (p. 79)

2. See Him for Who He Really Is (p. 89)

3. Put Your Happiness First (p. 107)

"It's Not My Fault"

At least, that is what he wants you to think.

He is not going to come right out and say it. Instead, he will come up with a bazillion reasons why he acted like a jerk. In essence, he's saying, "My tough breaks are your problem." Don't be fooled! His excuses may sound reasonable and may evoke sympathy, but on further inspection you will see that they set you up for more hurt.

This section details some of the most common excuses I have heard over the years for the bad behavior of Exes.

▶ Excuse #1: "It's My Ex's Fault"

His ex-girlfriend or ex-wife was controlling, unfaithful, needy, abusive, etc., and he is still recovering from her. So, it is really *her* fault that he has done bad things to you.

Many women hate their boyfriend's or husband's ex-partner and blame her for the raw deal they are getting from him. Ladies, let's direct this anger where it belongs! Chances are if he is driving you crazy, he drove all his other Exes crazy, too. His Ex may have been a piece of work, but he chose her, and if he's got some bad habits, rest assured they didn't start with you.

When you are dating someone who you know has a dark side and he makes a habit of bashing his Ex, it predicts what he will one day say about you. In reality, he may be talking trash about his Ex because he is still pissed that she didn't think he was the cat's pajamas and didn't stick around for what he dished out. Rather than hate his Ex, you might want to send her a sympathy card. You know exactly what she put up with, and it probably hurt her as much as it hurt you. A healthy partner may not like all of his Exes, but he doesn't use them as excuses.

▶ Excuse #2: "Things Are Tough at Work"

His job is hard or he has the boss from hell. Or maybe he lost his job. That is why he is so stressed out and why he treated you badly. I think pretty much everyone who has had a job has had job problems. It is normal to lean on your partner for support during tough times, and it is inevitable that sometimes a bad day at work can lead you to snap at the people you love. No one is perfect. But if his job problems have led to your overall dissatisfaction with the relationship, then your partner has not correctly managed this aspect of his life. Equally likely is that his bad behavior in the relationship is not really about the job at all. The job is just a convenient excuse and one he thinks you will buy. Even if he were to have another job—a great job—he would still treat you poorly and just use a different excuse.

▶ Excuse #3: "It Was My Fear of Commitment"

He had a fear of commitment that now he has miraculously gotten over. Many Exes who choose not to open themselves up to your love or to increased commitment or marriage use this excuse. You are supposed to believe that his fear is to blame for why things didn't work out. Some people really do fear intimacy and need their partners' patience and support to overcome this feeling. But if they know this about themselves, as they often do, and if they genuinely want to get past their fear, then they should be in some sort of counseling and actively working to resolve the issue so that you and the relationship don't suffer. They should bend over backward to make sure that their problem isn't your problem. What I see most often from hurtful Exes is that they only bring up this fear when it is convenient for them, and they don't do so in a way that might truly address this deep emotional issue.

▶ Excuse #4: "I Had a Rough Childhood"

I think this is the toughest excuse to protect yourself from, because there is an element of truth in it. We all play out and repeat some of the behaviors we saw growing up. If you witnessed dysfunction on the part of your parents or caregivers, you may find it incredibly difficult to have healthy relationships as an adult. But statistics show that even children who grow up being emotionally and physically abused usually do not go on to repeat those patterns in their adult relationships. It may take counseling, spiritual practice, or iron-will determination to keep from continuing the cycles we experienced growing up, but as adults those options are open to us. If you have a problem treating your partners well and you don't do anything about it, then you are the jerk and no one deserves to be your emotional punching bag. *It is not our God-given right to be in a relationship. We earn the privilege every day by being good to our partners.* And that is why this excuse really doesn't hold up.

❯ Excuse #5: "There Was a Death in My Family"

Grief can certainly change a person. When someone important in our life dies, we may go through an intense struggle. We may be depressed, be quick to anger, lose sleep, and experience other psychological and biological responses. Usually the symptoms lessen over time, although we may always feel some pain connected with the loss. I have never worked with a woman who left her partner soon after someone important to the partner died. In some cases they remained with the partner for years afterward. Whatever time had elapsed, Exes who like to rely on this excuse still pointed to the loss they'd suffered as the reason why things went south. Although a loved one's passing can be devastating—whether it was the loss of a beloved uncle or the death of a parent as a youngster—it does not give you a free pass to treat others poorly for the rest of your life. Don't feel bad about calling B.S. on this excuse. Whether your Ex knows it or not, it is a low-down, dirty trick to use someone's death to talk you into accepting less than you deserve. And the person who died is never coming back, so don't expect his reliance on this excuse—or his behavior—to change.

❯ Excuse #6: "My Finances Are Stressing Me Out"

Unless you are rich, dealing with bills and financial matters is not fun. To be clear, if you have children, a mortgage or lease, or other responsibilities, remember that it was your choice to have them—complete with both the benefits *and* the drawbacks. The drawbacks might include pressure to meet your financial obligations. Almost everyone you see around you is living with this downside and managing it.

When your Ex blames his lack of money or his attempts to get more money for his actions, he is basically admitting that he cannot do what many people do successfully, which is manage their finances. This is troubling for two reasons. First, being with someone who finds it difficult to manage his money is risky, especially if one day your money might be mixed up with his. Second, even if he managed to get out from under his financial worries, the truth is he would still act hurtfully toward you, except next time it would be because he had a tough day at work or because his mother was getting on his back about something. If he is the kind of person who feels comfortable taking out his bad mood on others, then he will always have a good reason to treat others poorly.

▶ Excuse #7: "My Last Breakup Messed Me Up"

This is a variation on Excuse #1. The same logic applies here. Things in our past can hurt us and make us reluctant to trust or love again. An ugly divorce or separation may give us some emotional baggage that unfortunately our next partner will have to deal with. But if your Ex's divorce or separation is such a big force in his life that it has driven you away from him, that is his fault. Healthy people may have pain around their divorce/separation/breakup, or wish that things had been different, but they don't revisit the horrors they went through on the next person unlucky enough to be with them. If they do, they deserve to be left—not as punishment but because their partner shouldn't have to suffer, too.

▶ Excuse #8: "My Kids Are Overwhelming"

Is it a surprise to anyone that raising children is stressful? It is also fulfilling and rewarding, but when things went well in your relationship, did your Ex ever say it was because of the kids? No, the kiddos get the blame only when things go poorly. That hardly seems fair. The truth is that although there can be times when our kids make us batty, they are not responsible for how we treat our partners.

▶ Excuse #9: "It's Because of My Problems with Alcohol/Drugs"

I have heard this one a lot, and it works pretty well to get bad guys out of trouble. It is often followed by the Ex's promise to decrease or cut out entirely his use of the troublesome substances. Not surprisingly, alcohol and drugs don't make things better in relationships. I have never had a client tell me, "My relationship was headed down the tubes until I started drinking every day." Rather, these substances usually intensify already existing issues. But I have seen many instances where even if the Ex stops using (and this is a big "if"; most Exes fail to rein in their addictions for longer than a few weeks), he still has the same personality and behaves in the same hurtful way as before. Only now he can't use the same excuse, because the addictive substance is gone. So the excuse changes to something else, and his partner is in the same unhappy situation she was in before. This is a big, fat trap.

Remember, too, that your Ex continues to make decisions when he is drunk or high. I have heard of many occasions when an Ex was acting crazy, supposedly because he had been using alcohol or drugs, but when the police, a family member, or someone else he wanted to hide his addiction from showed up, he suddenly stopped his wild behavior. He turned on the charm and apologized for what he had done. If he can control himself around these people, why can't he do it around you?

Consider whether what was happening to my client Isabel may also have been going on in your relationship. Isabel's Ex Jordan used to drink and then become angry and insulting toward her. Initially Isabel thought it was the drinking that sparked his temper. It wasn't until further reflection that she remembered that Jordan would seem to be upset or tense about something first, then drink, then verbally harass her. This was important information and helped Isabel to know that instead of the alcohol causing the outburst, it was the other way around. Jordan was mad to start with. The alcohol was just part of a ritual he had created that gave him "permission" and a good excuse for treating Isabel badly.

▶ Excuse #10: "I Can't Control My Anger"

This is an interesting one. In a way, your Ex is taking the blame, but in another way he's deflecting it. By saying he has a "problem," he is kind of admitting to something and at the same time using it as a crutch. It is almost like he expects you to say, "Oh, you have an anger control problem. Poor thing, go ahead and take it out on me." The more appropriate response is something like, "You have an anger control problem. What a coincidence. I have an I-don't-put-up-with-other-people's-crap problem. I guess you will have to find someone else to date."

Just saying you have a problem does not mean you escape the consequences. If this worked, then how about saying, "I have a paying-my-taxes problem." Or maybe a "cheating-with-my-friend's-husband problem." I am sure the IRS and my girlfriends would love that.

Here is a revealing exercise to help you see how ridiculous and easy it is for your Ex to use the "It's Not My Fault" tactic.

Self-Discovery Exercise #4: Excuses, Excuses

Read the sentence below, and fill in the blanks from the options that are listed beneath it. Use excuses you have heard your Ex make.

I am so sorry I treated you badly. If only I hadn't
_____ *and* _____,
I would have been able to be a much better boyfriend/husband to you. It won't happen again. Can I have another chance?

1. had a bad day at work
2. had so much to drink/gotten high
3. been disrespected by my boss
4. felt so sick
5. been so frustrated by traffic
6. had such a rough childhood
7. gotten that big bill I can't pay
8. had to talk to my ex-wife
9. gone through that nasty divorce
10. been sassed by the kids
11. lost control of my temper
12. lost my mother at such a young age

The exercise offers a simplified way of looking at this very serious and potentially harmful maneuver. And it shows how any of us can make excuses for our failure to be a good partner. *This exercise also shows that the real reason why your Ex was a poor partner is because he was willing to use excuses instead of taking responsibility and doing something about his hardships.* No relationship or life is perfect. That is an unobtainable goal. But a goal we can reach is to treat the people we love with respect and kindness no matter what kind of hand life deals us.

Although the sorts of issues outlined above can impact someone, they don't *make* that person behave in hurtful ways. You still choose how you focus your energy on a daily basis, the words you say to other people, and the love you share. If you hear these excuses, instead of being drawn into empathizer mode, I want you to think to yourself (or even say to him), "You need to call 1-800-I-Don't-Give-a-Crap," because despite what he wants you to believe, his issues are *not* your problem. No one gets through this life without getting some scars. I am sure you have faced your share of hardship, too. What it means to be an adult is that you alone are responsible for your actions, regardless of the tough breaks you've endured. You had a rough childhood. Go to a counselor. You have a bad boss. Get a new job, or just deal with it. You dated someone who treated you poorly—that means you know how it feels, so don't go and do that to someone else.

Most children understand the concept of treating others as they would like to be treated. Your Ex is hoping you will forget this basic life principle, focus on *his* pain and suffering, and overlook how much pain and suffering he caused you. As you heal from your hurt, don't forget where it came from, and don't forget that there will probably be more waiting for you if you go back to your Ex.

I know this can be tough. It can be incredibly tempting to want to help your Ex, offer him a shoulder to cry on, or try to love him out of whatever he has been through. Chances are you have already tried. Now the time for focusing on him is over. As they say, "That ship has sailed." *You already gave it your best, and your best is not what he needs. This does not mean there is something wrong with you; it means there is something wrong with him.*

While it may be comforting to think that your relationship ended due to outside forces, this is rarely the case. Yes, stressors large and small, such as jobs, money, or even the frustration of daily traffic, must be effectively managed within a relationship. If your Ex is incapable of doing that, then all his relationships are doomed unless he finds someone who will put up with being treated badly over and over. That is too heavy a price to pay, and I don't want you to be that person. Do not sacrifice yourself because of bad things that have happened to him. The only outcome would be two miserable people instead of one.

It is important to remember that your Ex is going to use the excuses that he believes you will be most susceptible to. If he has seen that you have a soft spot for his struggles with alcohol, or if he knows you can relate to his hard childhood, then these are the justifications he will utilize. If he has won you back before by playing the "my issues with anger control are the root of all our problems" card, then he will not hesitate to trot that one out. And the kinder you are to him, the thicker he will lay it on about how hard things have been for him. I have heard big, tough-guy Exes cry like babies to convince a woman how much they have struggled. If you cannot stand to see him cry, be on your guard. Knowing in advance that it can happen can help you be prepared for it.

Please know that your Ex may *genuinely believe* that his problems are to blame for his failure to be a good partner. Crediting outside influences for our behavior is still encouraged in our society. "Why did you steal from the company?" "Because I have a gambling addiction." "Why did you cheat on your wife?" "Because I have trust issues." "Why did you hit your kid?" "Because I was hit as a kid." People use these excuses—in daily life, in the media, and in court—because they work. When your Ex tells you that his tough breaks made him take it out on you, he may be very convincing. That's because he may even have convinced himself. Your seeing through his faulty logic will shock him, especially if this tactic has worked in the past or if others have cut him slack for the same reasons. Just because he is deluded about his responsibility for his actions does not mean that you have to be. If you go back, in essence you will be agreeing with him that he isn't responsible for his own behavior. Once this agreement is established, it will be open season on you whenever he feels pressure from life or just needs a convenient place to dump his toxic B.S.

Eventually, he might even be able to get you to make these excuses for him. I have heard countless women using excuses like the ones listed above for their Exes' bad behaviors because they've been talked into believing the excuses. If you hear yourself making excuses for your Ex, take a moment to think about why you are doing so and what it can mean for your efforts to stay gone from him. Once you start excusing the hurt he caused you, you will find it very difficult to remember why it is so important for you to keep away. At that point, his tough breaks will no longer be merely a problem you both share. They will be the rope that binds you to a man who freely chooses to hurt you.

1. Test His Words (p. 86)

2. Use a Freedom Journal (p. 87)

2. Don't Use the "Good Man" Excuse (p. 90)

"I Know All Your Secrets"

Who knows you better than anyone? For many of us it is the person we are dating or married to. One of the big bonuses of being in a relationship is having someone to whom we can tell everything—the good stuff, the bad stuff, the everything-in-between stuff. We share our insecurities, hopes, screw-ups, dreams, disappointments, and fears in the spirit of developing a bond with a person who will accept us just the way we are. And we can't know if they accept us unconditionally until we dish out all our dirt and see if they still hang around.

A huge amount of trust is required to reveal private information about ourselves to another: the guy in high school you cheated on and how it made you feel; the fact that you still wonder if you deserve to be loved; the bad thing your parents did to you as a child; the fact that you've dreamed of getting married and having a family since you were a little girl; your insecurities about the way you look; the things that make you feel most loved/angry/sad/lonely/happy. We all have things about us that we don't broadcast to everyone but do tell our partners. This is normal. It also means that most of our Exes have the goods on us in a big way. It is disturbing to think that a person would use our private information to manipulate us. But I have seen it often. When you leave a controlling or emotionally hurtful person, you are wrong if you think he will not use this "intel" to get what he wants.

You may say, "But how could my Ex use the fact that I told him how much I hate my thighs to manipulate me?" To that I reply there are literally a thousand ways to use that fact and others like it to deceive and hurt you. A story about Callie, one of my clients, illustrates this point. Callie and Alex had been dating for only about six months when she decided to call off the relationship. He was too controlling, was jealous, and had mood swings. Alex had pushed for the relationship to progress at a quick pace. Within the first three months Callie had moved in with him at his insistence, and they were on the fast track to getting married and starting a family. These were all things Callie really wanted—with the right man.

Early on, Callie told Alex that she didn't ever feel like she was able to be close to her father because of his drinking. This was hard for her to talk about because the feelings were so deep and painful.

After the breakup Alex kept calling to talk. Callie knew talking to him was a bad idea, but she felt sorry for him and was somewhat flattered by his persistence. During one conversation, Alex accused Callie of thinking all men were like her father and for playing out her family drama on him. He told her that he was a different kind of man (after all, he didn't even drink), and that he was willing to go see a counselor so they could figure out what part of their troubles were created by Callie's being the daughter of an alcoholic. He said he was willing to stick with her so she wouldn't have to be alone after always pushing men away.

Not surprisingly, this confused the heck out of Callie. On the one hand, she thought it was really mature and caring that

Alex would go to counseling to try to save the relationship. She wished her father had taken that option years ago. She also thought there might be some truth in Alex's accusation that she tended to keep men at arm's length to protect herself from being hurt the way she'd been by her father. And she really did harbor a fear that because of this tendency she ultimately would end up alone.

On the other hand, her gut instinct told her that her issues with her father were not why the relationship with Alex didn't work. In fact, as she talked to me, she described some behaviors on Alex's part that simply were not okay. For example, he was really jealous, and at times he questioned her repeatedly about where she had been, who she had been with, and what she had been doing. Or sometimes when he called her, she felt like he was trying to catch her doing something she wasn't supposed to.

I encouraged her to see that she was not dreaming up these incidents. They really did happen, and they were not remotely connected to her having an alcoholic father. *By concentrating on the concrete incidents and behaviors* that drove them apart, Callie was able to separate what she considered her "baggage" from Alex's unacceptable conduct. I had Callie make a journal of all the "not okay" things Alex had done since the beginning of the relationship.

When she started to doubt her decision to leave Alex, I asked her to look in that journal and ask herself if the reason those specific incidents hurt her was because her dad was an alcoholic. For example, one of the questions she asked herself was, "When Alex called you a liar because you didn't tell him you were going to lunch with a friend and he showed up at your work and you weren't there, did it hurt you because your dad is an alcoholic?" The answer was no. She realized that the reason why Alex's actions hurt her was because they would have hurt anyone! It became clear that Alex's focus on her dad's alcoholism was a way for him to distract Callie from the truth: that Alex was to blame for what he had done, not Callie or Callie's father. And the reason Callie pushed him away was because he was not good to her or for her.

If Callie had accepted Alex's version of the truth, she would have believed that she was the one with the problem, and Alex would have continued to use her emotional pain from being the child of an alcoholic, her tendency to move slowly with men, and her fear of being alone to keep her chained to him.

Think about it. What have you told your Ex that he might resurrect and use for his own benefit? Take a minute to write a few of them below.

Self-Discovery Exercise #5:
Your Ex's "Intel"

Old Hurts: _____

_____

Fears: _____

_____

Dreams: _____

_____

Insecurities: _____

_____

These personal subjects are no doubt close to your heart. By referring to them in certain ways, your Ex can hold great emotional sway over your decision-making without your even being fully aware of it. If your Ex brings up these matters in conversation, you should be on high alert. This is an extremely common and sneaky tactic for getting you back. You also need to know that your Ex may introduce these emotionally charged topics either in a hostile and aggressive way or in a seemingly sweet and innocent way. Be prepared for him to use some combination of both techniques.

Here's an example of the aggressive approach: "It was always your fault that I looked at other women. If you weren't so self-conscious about your body I wouldn't have had to." A statement like this can be very effective in jolting a person into feeling guilty for something that is definitely not her fault. And that is *why* an Ex will use it. Perhaps his partner opened up to him about not feeling sexy, not wanting to do certain things sexually, or feeling self-conscious about one of her body parts.

Here's another one: "If you weren't depressed all the time, I would want to spend more time with you." Why would he say that? You guessed it: Because you told him that you have been feeling down, or that you are thinking of seeing a counselor, or that you wonder if you need antidepressants (and who wouldn't after being with a guy like that).

A trickier Ex might sugar-coat his statements: "I know you always wanted a family, and I can give you that." Or, "You are the only one who understands me, because we both had alcoholic fathers." Both of these statements bring the partner's most personal information into play in an attempt to get her to return to the relationship.

Whether your Ex takes the hostile approach or the sweet and vulnerable one to use your confidences against you—or both—if you are tuned in you will catch him in the act. He knows you inside and out, and that makes him really dangerous. He knows which buttons to push and which ones to leave alone. Do not underestimate his cleverness in manipulating you!

1. Cut Off Communication (p. 79)

2. Test His Words (p. 86)

3. Use a Freedom Journal (p. 87)

"I Just Want to Be Friends"

The words sound innocent enough, and a lot of Exes and the women who left them end up saying this at some point after a relationship is over. True, people who once dated can sometimes remain friends, but very rarely does that happen when one partner has repeatedly hurt and/or manipulated the other. In that case, his invitation for friendship is most likely a setup to get you back. My suggestion is that you make friends with people who don't have such a huge potential to cause you harm…yet again.

Maybe you're tempted to think that remaining friends with your Ex is the kind thing to do, or that it will help him or you emotionally to slowly sever the ties to each other. Maybe you think you can let your Ex down easily.

When it comes to leaving a destructive relationship, I am a big fan of ripping the Band-Aid off whenever possible. The longer you continue to communicate with and be around your Ex, even as a friend, the more likely you are to fall back into a relationship with him, which may in fact be his plan. When other tactics to get you back haven't worked, be on the lookout for phrases like "Let's be friends," or, "Doesn't everything we've been through mean anything to you? We should at least be friends," or, "I don't think I can go on if we can't at least be friends." His goal is to keep you in his life to some degree—to prevent you from making a clean break.

This play can be very effective for a number of reasons, including the following ones:

1. Women feel guilty for saying no to this request. Your Ex knows this and will use your empathy against you. You can be kind and still say no to this request. In fact, *the kindest thing you can do for both yourself and your Ex is to tell him you cannot be friends. It sends him a clear message that he needs to move on, and it gives you the space and time you need to heal.* The more you allow him in your life as a friend or anything else, the harder it will be to get him to stop working to get you back, and that is not good for either of you.

2. Women don't want to hurt their Ex's feelings any more than they already have. This happens when the woman fails to understand whose fault the breakup was. Yes, you acted to end it, but it was his behaviors that led you to your decision. Don't feel bad for him now that he must face the consequences. Breakups are never fun; in fact, they stink, usually for both people involved. Remind yourself that he played a major part in this situation.

Keeping him in your life equals playing with fire. Don't sacrifice any more of yourself or your chances of a happy future to look out for his feelings. *He needs to be responsible for his feelings and actions, not you. That is the benefit of the breakup: you no longer have to fill that role.* Let yourself enjoy this freedom. It has been hard-won. No matter how much he says he is hurting or tries to play on your emotions, know that you are completely justified in looking out for yourself. Save your energy for helping *yourself* move on instead of focusing on how to make him feel better. The truth is you cannot make him happy; unless you are willing to martyr yourself. Both you and he must learn to deal with his disappointment.

3. Women think that being friends is really all he wants and that it may work out okay. Some women naïvely believe that their Ex really does just want an innocent friendship. They hope that even though he was a crappy intimate partner, he might still make a good friend. In fact, there may be lots of reasons why your Ex wants to be "friends" that are not innocent and have nothing to do with friendship.

For starters, by keeping you as a friend he can keep track of you, know if you are dating, and know how your life is going. This gives him certain advantages in the battle for your affection. Say he finds out that you had a rough day at work, or even that you had a death in the family. He might see this as a good time to offer you support—encouraging you to trust him and to build emotional dependence on him—all with the intention of getting you back. When you are grieving or feeling emotionally vulnerable and needy, you are not at your strongest to defend against the temptation to return to your Ex.

Please know that your moments of weakness, when a true friend would never take advantage of you, may be exactly when your Ex decides to make his move. I have seen situations in which Exes have hung around as "friends," creating problems, sometimes even in their former partner's new dating relationships. Yes, this is despicable behavior, and you probably hate to imagine that your Ex is capable of it, but why take the chance with something as important as your happiness? You must save your trust and friendship for those who have proven themselves worthy of it. Your Ex has demonstrated that he is not.

4. Women think they owe friendship to their Ex. It is a terrible fact that some women believe that their Exes have a right to demand to be friends with them, and that they are "mean" if they don't agree to it. This couldn't be less true. But some women have been made to believe that because they once loved this person, or because of the things they went through together, they are obliged to continue to show love, caring, and even affection after the breakup. Remind yourself that ending those commitments is what a breakup is all about! You broke up with him so that each of you could move on. If you still feel obligated to your Ex, if you still believe that you owe him something, then he still has power over you. That means you remain bound to him and continue to sacrifice your independence and emotional freedom.

Think about it: Is it more humane for you to break things off a second time, once you realize you need to end the friendship (which is almost certainly inevitable)? Don't cause additional stress and heartache for yourself and your Ex that could have been avoided if you'd stood by your guns and refused to be friends in the first place. By the way, here is how you tell an Ex you don't want to be friends with him; "Edward, I cannot be friends with you." Notice that you do not have to tell him why, rehash the past, or negotiate this in any way.

5. Women miss their Ex and think that being friends would help. I know how badly it hurts to leave someone you love but cannot be with. Trying to be friends with your Ex can be a desperate attempt to ease your pain. The first thing to remember if you are missing your Ex is that there are many ways to help yourself feel better that are preferable to being his friend. Review the suggestions that are mentioned in the section "The L Word: Loneliness," on page 140.

Becoming friends with your Ex is the worst thing you can do to cure this longing. To believe that it might work to let him back into your life while simply swapping the title "boyfriend" or "husband" for "friend" is like an alcoholic trying to quit drinking by pouring some lovely merlot, swirling it around the glass, inhaling its fragrance, and keeping it in a place where she can see it all day. To be that close to the very thing she desires would be torture. It would definitely not be a good strategy for staying sober. Likewise, being "just friends" with your Ex is not a good way to stay broken up with him. If you are around your Ex—seeing him, listening to him, hearing about his day and letting him know about yours—the temptation to get back with him may overwhelm your good judgment. You may just grab that merlot and chug it down. You'll regret it later when the "hangover" hits because you realize he is the same Ex and your relationship has the same problems. Better to sidestep the slip-up entirely and avoid even letting yourself be tempted.

1. Cut Off Communication (p. 79)

2. Use a Freedom Journal (p. 87)

3. Mourn the Loss of the Salesman (p. 105)

"What About the Children?"

Even if you do not have children, reading this section may offer insight into the manipulative behaviors of some Exes. Anytime children are in the picture, the stakes are higher. Our little ones depend on us entirely to keep them safe and to meet their needs. Moms in general take this responsibility very seriously. I have little doubt that if your Ex were to hurt your children outright, either emotionally or physically, the mama bear in you would want to come roaring out and rip him to shreds. Your Ex knows this, too. Chances are he won't deliberately hurt your kids. In fact, he may love them very much and genuinely miss them or want the best for them. If he is the kind of man who you even suspect has or would verbally, physically, or sexually abuse a child, please seek help from police, child protective services, or the Childhelp National Child Abuse Hotline at (800) 4-A-CHILD (800-422-4453), and make full use of your legal rights. Also consider calling a crisis hotline or domestic violence shelter for information and recommendations (see the Resources section at the back of the book).

What is more common is for an Ex to use the children in certain subtle ways to try to get you to come back to him. He may honestly believe that remaining together as a couple is the best thing for you and the kids, so he rationalizes his actions. Let me be clear that this manipulative behavior is a terrible thing to do to a child and her or his mother; it only causes additional pain for everyone during what is already a difficult time. But your Ex may not see the damage he is doing, he may feel he is doing it for a good reason, or he may believe that his manipulations aren't that bad.

An Ex will typically use children to get to you in two different ways. The first is to use your love for your children to manipulate you. The second is to directly involve the children in his efforts to communicate with you.

Under scenario one, your Ex may pull at your heartstrings by saying, "We can be a family," or, "Don't you want your child to have a father?" *If I were to pinpoint one tactic used by Exes that is the most effective in causing women to return to destructive relationships, this one is it!* Colleagues of mine say the same thing.

Here is how it works. Your Ex will make a statement like, "Don't you want us to be a family?" Or, "Don't you think it is important for little Timmy to have a dad?" Or, "We've got to make this work for the kids." He repeats this message often to make you feel like you are tearing the family apart and damaging your child. Oh how cold and unfeeling you must be not to run back into his arms for the sake of the children. In fact, however, he knows that you, like most women, would do almost anything you can think of to create the close family you know your children deserve. That's why he's playing on this sensitive area. Of course you want to have a great family, provide your child with a loving male role model, and have stability and safety in the home. There is no question here. Almost every woman wants this. And if that is really what your Ex were offering, then I would advise you to go back to him. But you wouldn't have left in the first place if things were great or even just okay. No, something was really wrong.

Chances are both you and your children have been negatively impacted by your Ex or by the dysfunction of the relationship, and just like a mother bear, you have to protect them from this harm. Know that there are men out there who will deliver on the promise of a warm, loving family and not just use it to manipulate you into staying.

As a final note, women who grew up without a father seem especially vulnerable to this tactic. Perhaps they've pledged to provide their children with the father they never had. This is a very worthy goal. Good fathers are incredibly important. But you cannot let this dream for your children keep you hostage to a man whom you know you need to leave. In many cases the benefits to the children of having a father are outweighed by the negative traits they pick up from a disrespectful, hurtful, or abusive father, as well as by the guilt that can arise from their knowing you are sacrificing your happiness for them. *From my experience, the children always know when mom is staying in a bad relationship for them, even if they are never told so directly.*

Here's another tactic your Ex might employ: "I miss the kids so much." Hearing this will probably be painful, especially if your children are also telling you that they miss your Ex.

A breakup is hard. There's no getting around it. It's hard on you, your Ex, and your children. All of you will likely experience legitimate feelings of loss. Be on alert for his playing on these emotions and holding you responsible for them. Be prepared for statements like, "Why are you doing this?" Or promises about how he'll take the kids someplace special, or dredging up memories about good times he's had with the kids. These types of things can be really hard to hear.

No doubt you hate to deprive your children and your Ex of each other's company and love. Only *you* know what the right boundaries are between you, your Ex, and your children. You have to be firm about these rules. Don't be tempted to remove certain boundaries simply because you feel sorry for your Ex. Eliminating boundaries, negotiating about the kids, or communicating too often about the kids can give your Ex more chances to talk you into returning to him. Remind yourself that you deserve to be happy, and that your Ex had lots of opportunities to treat you right. He made choices that ultimately led to this situation, painful as it may be for him. In the counseling profession we call these "natural consequences." When you make certain choices, you face certain consequences. In his case, separation from you and the children is a consequence of how your Ex behaved in the relationship.

Throughout this difficult transition, your kids will be looking to you for guidance, emotional support, and most of all a consistent message about what role, if any, your Ex will play in their lives. Your consistency will provide them with reassuring structure and with the information they need to adjust to the new situation. It can be very harmful for the rules or boundaries around your Ex's interaction with the children to change weekly or monthly.

Again, this can be a very delicate and emotional time for everyone. Your children may cry and beg you to get back together with your Ex, even if he has hurt you or them. This can be upsetting and may cause you to question your decision to leave. What mom wants to feel as though she's causing her children pain? Children can be very persistent and convincing when they want something. As the parent, you are responsible for deciding what is best for them and for you. Children's feelings are very important, of course, but their reasoning and understanding of the situation between you and your Ex is not at an adult level. Do not let them make the decision for you because you don't know how to put your foot down and do what *you* believe is best. You don't allow your kids to eat candy and French fries at every meal. You know they need balanced nutrition, and so at times you probably make them eat food they think is gross. Likewise, trust that you know what is best for them emotionally, which may mean setting limits around your Ex that they dislike.

If you feel nervous about your ability to talk to your children about what has happened between you and your Ex and about how things will look moving forward, utilize resources such as family or individual counseling, or brainstorm with a wise and trusted friend or relative.

In the second scenario, your Ex may use your children directly in his attempts to get you back. He may send messages to you through the children, or he may get information about you from them. He may tell the kids how much he misses their mommy and ask them to relay his pleadings to you. He may ask them questions about you, like whether you are dating anyone. Don't assume that your Ex would never stoop this low. I've witnessed it many times.

This ploy of your Ex's presents challenges on several levels. It may make you feel sorry for your Ex, pissed at him for manipulating the children, or sad for your kids who innocently deliver the messages. Any of these feelings could tempt you to talk to your Ex about the situation. Be careful here! Again, any time you talk to your Ex—even just to tell him to leave the kids alone—you are offering him a chance to make his case for you to go back to him. Think carefully before contacting him. Maybe you could ask a third party to tell him that you expect him to keep all the relationship talk separate from the children. Another, perhaps better, option is to comfort your children as best you can, explain in an age-appropriate way what is happening, and ignore his manipulations.

If your Ex keeps up this behavior, and if it is in your power to remove the children from this situation or modify the visitation arrangements, you may want to consider or work toward these arrangements. You and your children deserve peace of mind, and if your Ex will not let you have it, then you need to do whatever it takes to separate yourself and your family from him. This is not only your right; it is your duty as a parent.

1. Reclaim Your Instincts (p. 88)
2. Mum's the Word (p. 95)
3. Put Your Happiness First (p. 107)

"You're Going to Be Sorry"

The scare tactics discussed in this section take things up a notch. By using them, your Ex means to frighten you and possibly even hurt you. Tragically, even a professed love for a former partner doesn't stop a certain kind of man from intimidating, threatening, or taking action to hurt her. And some women are convinced or bullied into going back to their Exes by these methods.

▶ **Scare Tactic #1: "You'll Never Find Another Man"**
Here are some variations:

- "You'll never find anyone as good as me."
- "I was the best thing that ever happened to you."
- "One day you'll be sorry you did this."
- "Next week you'll be begging me to take you back."
- "You're going to be old and alone."

Or maybe he'll tap into your insecurities: "No other man

will want to be with a woman with two kids/a big butt/a lot of debt...."

These are really nasty thoughts for your Ex to plant in your head, and each one is strategically intended to make you lose confidence in your decision to leave.

▶ Scare Tactic #2: "You Won't Be Able to Make It on Your Own"

Variations include:

- "How do you think you are going to pay the bills?"
- "You know you need me to take care of you."
- "You're so naïve. Everyone is going to take advantage of you."

Each of these statements seeks to highlight one of your vulnerabilities and use it to make you believe that you will fail in your attempt to leave, or that you will be miserable without him.

▶ Scare Tactic #3: "I Won't Let You Leave Me"

Other variations:

- "Only I can say when this is over."
- "You don't tell me when we're done. I will tell you!"

Statements like this reveal how truly controlling and delusional certain Exes are. Some men believe that they must give you permission to break up with them, or that they are the only ones who can end the relationship.

It is particularly important to cut off communication with an Ex who says things like this. He may mightily resist believing that you have ended things, he may be extra pushy in his attempts to get you back, or he may try to punish you for leaving. *Never forget that you get to decide whom you want to have in your life. No matter what your Ex says, this is your right and you must protect it.* Anyone who really cares about you, let alone loves you, will want you to freely choose them, not stay with them because you are coerced to.

▶ Scare Tactic #4: "I Will Make You Regret Leaving Me"

In this case, your Ex is using fear instead of love to get you back. Specifically, he's using your fear that he will hurt you if you don't return to him. Here is a list of things Exes may do or threaten to do if this is their chosen tactic:

- start gossip or rumors about you with friends or family
- call your place of work to start trouble
- make a threat against you, your family, or your friends
- follow you, watch you, or try to collect information about you, with or without telling you that they are doing so
- damage, steal, or sell your property
- start a legal action against you, or report something to police
- tell your children lies about you
- harass you by telephone, e-mail, or in another way
- yell at you and call you names
- try to hurt you financially
- hurt your pets
- become physically or sexually abusive or violent toward you

As you can see, some Exes' attempts to punish or threaten you can range from frightening to deadly. Only a small percentage of Exes will go so far as to do these things, but the ones who do are dangerous. *They are dangerous because these behaviors demonstrate how entitled they feel to hurt others in order to get what they want.* And then the question becomes how far will they go? That is not a question you want to stick around to learn the answer to.

You cannot prevent your Ex from engaging in controlling, intimidating conduct. But you can prepare yourself for the possibility that he will. First, trust your gut about his potential for doing so. If he has ever acted in a threatening manner toward you or anyone else, then you know that he is capable of doing so and is likely to do so again. A man who is controlling, jealous, or lacks empathy for others is also a likely candidate for behaving in this disturbing way.

You may be able to shrug off some of the deeds listed above, like starting rumors. Others, like making threats, following you, harassing you, or hurting you physically, are against the law. They require attention and vigilance on your part, and perhaps police intervention. Even if you decide not to report illegal behaviors, you can get support and ideas about how to protect yourself. My best suggestion is to call a domestic violence shelter. The National Domestic Violence Hotline can put you in touch with your local shelter: **(800) 799-SAFE (7233)**. Contact information is listed again in Resources, at the end of the book. You don't need to be looking for a shelter or be in a true crisis to call the hotline and get some questions answered. Nor will the person on the other end of the line try to convince you to take any certain action or judge what you tell them. They are required by law to keep your information confidential. And there's a good chance they will be able to answer your questions and give you ideas and options you haven't considered. Remember that domestic violence shelters are full of professionals who want to help you and who work with this difficult issue daily.

One very important point about scare tactics is that if you have the kind of Ex who will resort to them—and if you return to your Ex after he uses them—it dramatically increases the likelihood that he will use them again in the future. Furthermore, generally speaking, these men increase the frequency with which they rely on fear to get your compliance, and they increase the severity of their behavior. You can especially expect this to happen if you return and then begin to show a determination to leave again.

Unfortunately, even when Exes use unconscionable strategies such as these, it is often their partners who feel shamed into keeping their abusive behavior a secret. *Secrets like these are very dangerous. It is not your fault if your Ex is doing these things; don't be afraid to reach out to people you trust for help.* The more willing a woman is to let others know what is happening, to seek out useful information, and to use the sorts of strategies suggested in this book, the more likely she is to be able to defend herself from scare tactics.

Lastly, if your Ex is engaging in these intimidating behaviors, let me say I am very sorry. I wish I could be there to support you and help you get through it, and I hope that through this book I am doing that in some small way. I am also sorry we live in a society where too often men can get away with these deeds. Please let this injustice only strengthen your resolve—and your commitment to your own freedom—because no woman deserves this kind of life.

A number of helpful organizations are listed in the back of the book, many of them created specifically to assist people who have current or former partners who use the type of controlling ploys outlined in this chapter. Please do not hesitate to contact these resources, particularly if you fear your Ex.

1. Reclaim Your Instincts (p. 88)

2. Don't Be There (p. 97)

3. Keep Your Eyes on the Prize (p. 106)

PART II

Surefire Strategies for X-ing Your Ex

X

4

Standing Behind Your Truth

Have you seen the animated Disney movie *The Lion King*? In the opening number, the newborn lion cub, Simba, is held overhead by the wise elder baboon, Rafiki, for all the animals to see. The sunlight is shining on baby Simba, the song "Circle of Life" is playing, and everyone is happy and in awe of their new prince. I want you to do the same thing with your truth—your truth about yourself, the relationship you ended, your reasons for not going back, what you are worth, the future you want—all of it. Hold it up as the marvelous and wonderful thing it is, and protect it with all you've got.

A lot of hard-won knowledge has gone into establishing your truth, and denying it puts you at a huge disadvantage to your Ex. You cannot disrespect or deny your truth without disrespecting or denying the most fundamental parts of yourself. That is why many of your Ex's tactics are designed to make you doubt yourself and your truth. If he can accomplish this—if he can make you an accomplice in destroying your truth—your resolve to stay away from him will eventually crumble. This chapter outlines seven concrete strategies you can use to uphold and honor your truth, even in the face of your Ex's attempts to discredit it.

Cut Off Communication

This one is easy to say and hard to do. But it's fundamental. If he can't talk to you, almost all of the tactics from his playbook will be completely useless. Still, many women find it very tempting to talk to their Ex after a breakup. A short time ago your lives were intertwined, and you developed patterns that necessitated talking to him. Maybe when you came home from work or had dinner together you told each other about your day. Checking in with each other is a healthy part of relationships that can help people feel supported.

After your breakup, you will probably crave having that other person around to talk to. At first, it may feel unnatural not to pick up the phone to call your Ex when something big happens. Women come up with lots of good reasons to call their Exes, but strategies exist for resisting that temptation. Consider it your job to utilize them.

In some cases, in spite of the many advantages to cutting off communication, a woman is unable to do so or will choose not to. Women who have children with their Ex, or who know they need more time to emotionally separate, or whose Ex uses scare tactics may find themselves in the difficult position of navigating the path to independence while keeping one foot in their Ex's world. If you find yourself in one of these situations the suggestions below may be helpful to you.

1. If you have a child or children with your Ex. Cutting off communication with your Ex may not be an option or may not be in your or your child's best interest. Only you can be the judge of whether this is true for you. If you need to have some contact with your Ex, by being thoughtful about how to proceed you can minimize any possible negative effects on you. Aim to strike a balance between working with your Ex to get your children's needs met and not opening the door to his verbal manipulations. If you feel your conversation drifting away from what you need to discuss for the children and into dangerous territory, have some ideas in mind about things you can say to refocus the discussion. Or just end it. Here are some ideas; you can come up with others: "John, I am having this conversation to talk about Tommy's daycare, not to rehash our relationship. I am happy to talk about what's going on with Tommy, or we can end this conversation." Or, "John, when you want to discuss Tommy's daycare you can call me back."

Don't be afraid to be firm with him about your boundaries around communication. You may need to reassert those boundaries more than once in multiple conversations before he gets it that you mean business and aren't negotiating or playing hard to get. Be prepared to follow through by, for example, hanging up the phone if your Ex refuses to respect your request for healthy communication. Being armed ahead of time by knowing what to say will help you in the moment when the conversation turns from a subject you are willing to discuss into one you are not.

2. If you cannot yet bring yourself to cut emotional ties with your Ex. Perhaps you are so emotionally connected to your Ex that you are not yet ready to end communication. In that case, limit your contact with him, and set a goal for decreasing it over time. This may mean putting yourself on a Facebook diet in which you avoid looking at his profile or messaging him every day and instead do it once a week. Or you can set a goal that by the end of the month you will not be talking or communicating with him anymore. Don't discount the importance of having strategies for stepping down your communication with your Ex. By deliberately adopting the intent to eventually cease contact, and setting interim goals toward that end, you can wean yourself off of potentially destructive behavior and feel good about the progress you are making.

One last caution: even small exchanges of information tend to generate the need for more exchanges, creating a harmful cycle of increasing contact. Say you look at your Ex's Facebook page and notice that his relationship status has changed from "Single" to "It's Complicated." Is this new information going to make you feel more grounded or more desperate, calmer or more anxious, happier or more upset? Will it increase your desire to contact him and get some answers, or will you be able to shrug it off as no big deal? Don't set yourself up for more disappointment, and don't give yourself a new reason to feel you must call, text, e-mail, flip him the bird, or in any other way communicate with him.

3. If your Ex uses scare tactics. Some women may feel they need to keep tabs on their Ex for their own safety. If this sounds like your situation, be sure to pay attention to the section "You're Going to Be Sorry," in Chapter 3 (page 72). It was written specifically for you. Your safety comes first, and you know best how to secure it. Still, be aware that if you communicate with your Ex, all of his weapons of verbal manipulation will be fully engaged and targeting you. You can overcome this disadvantage, but you will need to be prepared for what he might send your way, and you will need to line up a lot of support.

Speaking of support, *every* woman who has recently ended a destructive relationship should make it a priority to cultivate healthy relationships with people who will be there for her and listen to her. Connect with friends or relatives whom you trust, and don't be afraid to lean on them for support. If you simply go cold turkey from your Ex, and you don't have other friendships to sustain you, your feelings of desperation and loneliness may be too much to bear and may make you very vulnerable to going back to him.

Take Pride in Your Pride

I don't know if you remember much about Greek mythology. I don't—but I do remember that the humans were always being punished for having too much pride. Take the story of Icarus, whose father, Daedalus, made wings of wax and bird feathers. Before takeoff, Daedalus warned Icarus not to fly too close to the sun. But of course Icarus, overcome with the thrill of flight, flew higher and higher, until he was too close to the sun. The heat from the sun melted the wax in the wings, and Icarus fell to his horrible death. That seemed to be the moral of many Greek myths: Too much pride means you are headed for a fall.

I think that's B.S. To my mind, anyone who can make a set of wings and fly with them deserves to be proud. We receive lots of messages while growing up about the dangers of pride. We're taught that pride is the opposite of being humble or good. Pride has gotten a bad rap.

I stand in defense of pride. I am not talking about the pride that keeps you from apologizing when you should, or the pride that makes you look down on other people. No. Those are clearly bad versions of pride, but they're not the only kinds. We can call the version I am advocating "platinum pride." Platinum pride is a good name because this sort of pride is worth more to you than gold. It deserves to be recognized for the valuable tool it is, especially for women who have recently left unhealthy relationships. I have *never* talked to a woman who had left a hurtful partner and found myself thinking, "Boy, that lady would be far better off if she would just swallow her pride!" In fact, I usually think the opposite. If more women would turn to their pride when questioning or doubting themselves, it would lead them to the answers they seek, answers that would protect them.

Maybe you've found yourself wrestling with one or more of the following questions:

"Was breaking up with my partner the right thing to do?"

"Should I get back together with him now?"

"Are my feelings of anger or sadness over his behavior justified?"

"Was what he did really that bad?"

"Can we make this work?"

One of the definitions of "pride" in *Webster's Dictionary* is "a reasonable or justifiable self-respect." My own definition is similar but a little less academic: Pride is the part of you that won't tolerate certain crap—*period*. It tells you when your breaking point has been reached and exceeded.

Platinum pride does not buckle or seek others' approval. In a storm that washes everything else away, it stays with you. And it can be enough to rebuild on. During the rare times when someone *really* pushes you too far, your pride is sturdy enough to defend you. Your pride can keep you out of huge trouble; it can be the last line of defense between you and a soul-sucking relationship. When an Ex who hasn't treated you right injures your pride he has crossed the line. That is the kind of pride I am talking about.

Now tap into your platinum pride, and imagine your responses to the list of questions above. Platinum pride makes you say things like:

"Oh hell no, I am not putting up with that!"

"He must have thought he was dating someone else!"

"I will *never* let myself get in that situation again."

"Get your stuff and get out!"

"This is the last time you are going to treat me this way!"

"That guy is crazy. I'm outta here."

As you can see, platinum pride sends short, clear, unmistakable messages. It cusses and likes exclamation points. All the statements above are bold, decisive, and set clear boundaries. They leave no doubt about your course of action.

I've had the pleasure of hearing a number of shy, gentle, relatively passive women recount stories of what they told their Exes in "prideful" moments, and how completely shocked the Ex was to receive both barrels of that anger. Usually the only one more shocked than the Ex was the wife or girlfriend who did the blasting. Some of them didn't know that this powerful force was dwelling inside them, or that it was going to come out and kick some butt.

When this happens it can often lead to an emotional breakthrough that can set a woman on a path to greater freedom and happiness. When women tell these stories they almost always find themselves laughing deep belly laughs. Stories in which women stand up for themselves in dramatic fashion and take back the power or respect that had been denied them are always inspirational and exciting.

A colleague of mine, Ruth, once told me a story about how her pride expressed its certainty during her breakup from her abusive Ex. She had been fed up with how Antonio had treated her for some time, and she had been looking for the right time to leave him. Knowing that the end of the relationship was near and that Antonio would go berserk if he knew her plans, Ruth put things into place (housing, important documents, a reserve of cash) so that when the right day came she could just walk about the door—and that is just what she did. One day her pride told her that it was now or never. She asked Antonio what he wanted for dinner, he said "Chicken," and she left under the auspices that she was going to get take out. She never went back. She and her family still laugh about how long Antonio must have been waiting for his chicken.

Unfortunately, too many times after women have felt their pride well up and push them in a certain direction, they later second-guess it. They sometimes come to think that their bold, healthy response was something to be ashamed of. Feeling that fiery energy for the first time can be an alarming experience. Instead of trusting the amazing gift of clarity, they condemn the strength of their feelings or the way they expressed themselves as they grapple with their emotions and their Ex's reactions. This can happen minutes, days, or even months after the fact. They may decide that they were too mean, aggressive, or judgmental, or that they should have been more patient or a better person. It kills me when this happens, because a strong, instinctive, and pride-inspired response is a beautiful, self-protective gift. It should be celebrated when it shows up for the huge red flag that it is, and it should be respected by being acted on.

Certainly you don't want to respond this way to all situations, or lay into your partner without provocation, but that is almost never the case. Usually your injured pride flares up only after you have been repeatedly disrespected and are in danger of being further hurt and degraded. Your pride is the neon-red stop sign that can snap you back into reality.

Fortunately, healthy pride is very resilient and can survive being injured and overruled. But if you constantly suppress your pride so that you can forgive or be with someone who hurts you, eventually it will become less responsive. I have seen women who have acted against their pride or convinced themselves that their pride was getting in the way of their happiness so many times that they no longer notice their gut instinct when it tells them to leave. They stay, continuing to suffer through incredible insults.

Talking yourself out of what your pride tells you means that your boundaries will get pushed farther and farther back. Something that you never would have put up with before becomes just another part of your reality. In an internal tug-of-war, your healthy impulses are pulling you away from harmful people and situations, while your Ex is urging you in the opposite direction, toward an acceptance of his bad behaviors.

Eventually people get used to having their boundaries violated. Many women have spoken to me about this phenomenon by saying, "If you had told me at the beginning of the relationship what he was going to do to me, or the person I would become with him, I never would have believed it!" Or they'll say, "I would never want my daughter/sister/niece to be in a relationship like this." Women who repeatedly ignore their survival instincts get taken advantage of and lose some of their essential ability to stick up for themselves.

If this has happened to you, understand that your pride is now your best friend. Be willing to welcome and heed its messages. I've heard women say that although they were lonely, having financial difficulties, and their Ex was tempting them to come back, their pride refused to let them give up. Sometimes when we leave a relationship, our pride is all we leave with. But it is all we need to start again.

Test His Words

If you do end up talking to your Ex, put his words to the test. If he makes excuses for why he behaved the way he did, or if he uses your secrets to intimidate you, ask yourself the following two questions. Using a friend or a counselor as a sounding board for this process may help you to see that what your Ex says doesn't add up.

Do his statements make sense? Are they logical? In the story about Alex and Callie (Chapter 3), it didn't make sense that the bad things Alex did were a result of something from Callie's childhood, namely her dad's alcoholism. But she didn't realize that this was a manipulation on Alex's part until she took the time to deconstruct, analyze, and test what he was saying.

Would someone else be upset by my Ex's negative behaviors? Think about a woman whom you respect. What would she think about your Ex's bad deeds? Would she be impressed, or would she be out the door? If she would be bothered by your Ex's behaviors, then it totally makes sense that you would be, too.

Asking these questions can help you to diffuse some of the emotional charge triggered by his manipulative words. Then you can make decisions based on *your* truth, no matter what he believes or tries to convince you is true.

Use a Freedom Journal

This isn't your typical diary. In this journal I want you to list every crappy thing he did to you. I know this is a depressing way to spend a Saturday afternoon, and I would never ask you to do it if it weren't one of the most effective tools I can offer. Here is how to use this tool. When you are thinking about calling your Ex, read your journal. When he tries to put a spin on his bad behavior, read your journal. When he makes his case for why you should come back to him, read your journal. When he tries to convince you to be his friend, read your journal. When he tells you that you cannot make it without him, you guessed it—read your journal. Your journal will give you a much needed reality check when your Ex makes a play on your emotions or brings up your secrets.

Sometimes you need a good reminder of why you left your Ex, especially when he tries to get you all twisted up emotionally. Reading your journal will help you keep your feet planted firmly in *reality* and *truth*. The reality is that he was not good for you. And the truth is that you are not going back to him!

Reclaim Your Instincts

We all have gut feelings, delivered to us by that little voice that sometimes can be hard to hear. It may tell us, "Watch out, that person is dangerous," or, "I think this person is trying to con me." Making a habit of either listening to or ignoring our instincts determines whether or not we are able to stay in touch with them and keep ourselves safe physically and emotionally.

You may be out of practice hearing your inner messages, either because of your own behaviors or because your Ex may have encouraged you to override them. The result may be that you are not currently on speaking terms with this part of yourself. Don't worry—over time this inner voice will come back if you nurture and listen to it. That requires paying attention to what your body and mind are telling you. From now on, if you get a feeling that your Ex is up to no good, or you have a hunch that a decision you are making could put you at risk of returning to him, out of respect for your instincts take a step back and consider your alternatives.

Many people think that because our gut feelings aren't always based on facts, they should not be followed. But from my experience, your intuition will rarely steer you in the wrong direction. You must believe in yourself and your ability to figure out the right path. Your instincts can play an important role in that journey.

For more information about how your instincts can help keep you safe, see the listing for *The Gift of Fear* in the Resources section at the end of the book.

See Him for Who He Really Is

There are certain times in relationships when we are not ourselves—or at least not *completely* ourselves. We usually aren't totally ourselves at the beginning of a new relationship, or right after a relationship ends. On a first date, we are typically on our best behavior. We get all dolled up and show ourselves in the best light possible. We do this when we like the other person so that we can get to date number two. Think about it—if your Ex had displayed some of his less civilized behaviors on the first date by being blatantly jealous, critical, passive-aggressive, uncaring, argumentative, stingy, or cold, would you have even taken his next call? You probably would have thanked your lucky stars when the date ended and would have blocked his number from your phone. But that is not the way it worked out, mainly because people like your Ex know when they can show their true selves and when they need to mind their manners.

The same can be said for your Ex after a breakup. If he is trying to get you back he will be on his best behavior. You may wonder who he really is. Is he the great man you fell in love with or the man whose less appealing side began revealing itself a few months into the relationship?

Simply put, your Ex's real self is the person he has been since the newness of the relationship wore off. That is when he became comfortable enough to show you his true colors. *This is the personality he will most likely have for the rest of his life. If you didn't like this personality or your Ex's behaviors during your relationship, then you have made a wise decision to leave. Congratulate yourself.*

Now that you have left, your Ex is facing the challenge of getting you back. No wonder he is acting like a new and improved version of himself, just as he did when you first met. The big difference is now that he knows you, he will be able to customize what he says and does in ways that he thinks will win you back. You will need to be alert to such tactics and remind yourself that as quickly as frogs turn into princes, they can turn back into frogs again.

Don't Use the "Good Man" Excuse

When you hear the words "good man," what qualities do you think of? Take a minute to write a few of them down.

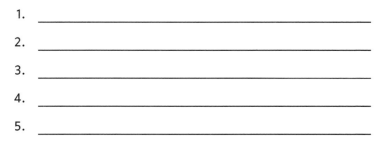

**Self-Discovery Exercise #6:
The Characteristics I Think a Good Man Has**

1. _____

2. _____

3. _____

4. _____

5. _____

This is a question that each woman will answer differently, but there is pretty consistent agreement on certain qualities. Most women will agree that a good man is at least loving, respectful, kind, faithful, loyal, and honest. A good man also has flaws, maybe some pretty deep ones, but he is at least these things.

I have noticed that I can make this list with a female client, and we can agree on some basic qualities of a good man, and even after we have decided together that her Ex *doesn't* meet this standard, she may still later say, "Oh, but he was a good man." How confusing. Why do we as women insist on calling our Exes "good men" even when there is lots of evidence to the contrary? And what does it mean for our chances to stay gone if we do?

Other statements women make that conceal the truth are: "Oh, but it wasn't that bad." "I know he never meant to hurt me." "I'm really fine." "I did a lot of bad things too." "No one is perfect." " Sure he had his problems, but he was the greatest father." "He could be so loving sometimes." "No one knows me better."

All of these statements tend to serve the same function. This section concentrates on how using the label "good man" can trip you up, but please know that if you are using any of the above statements they may be dangerous to you in the same way.

Let's start with an important question. Can someone be called a "good man" and yet cheat on you, disrespect you, consistently lie to you, withhold affection from you, not support you, mooch off you, or let his anger get out of control? I would say no. Any of these behaviors disqualify him from being called a good man. Men who do these things may not be monsters, but they certainly aren't good men.

Why am I making such a big deal about this? Three reasons. First, there really are good men out there. We cheapen their goodness when we call just anyone a good man. Good men deserve to get credit for living up to the basic standard described above. They shouldn't be lumped in with every guy who has a pulse. When women forget that guys exist who can live up to this standard and even surpass it, we tend to settle for less than we deserve. So whether you have encountered them or not, it is important to remember that there are good men out there. A lot of them.

The second reason is because women are taught that they should stay with a good man no matter what. Think of the saying "A good man is hard to find." It implies that if you can find a good one, you darn sure better hold on to him. When we mistakenly call our Exes "good men," it sets us up to think that we shouldn't throw the relationship away. On the contrary, we believe that if we don't make it work there must be something wrong with us. Or even that we'll be doomed to unhappiness with a not-so-good man.

Here's the final reason why we need to be clear about this "good man" designation. Often we call our Ex a good man only because we feel guilty for having left him. We also might be reacting to the sorrow we feel at having to finally face his negative qualities and the ways he hurt us. By calling our Ex a good man, we may be trying to minimize or gloss over our pain and guilt over the way things went down.

People are often unaware they're doing this. Sometimes I'll ask a client why she left her partner, and she'll reply, "The relationship had been bad for a long time. I kept hoping that I could make him change or that he would see how much I loved him, but he never did. He worked all the time and was really just checked out. He never complimented me and often made me think that I was asking for too much. He also had a way of making me feel like I was never good enough." (Brief pause.) "But you know, he was a good man."

When I hear this, the unprofessional side of me wants to scream, "No, he *wasn't* a good man to you. He was a jerk and you didn't deserve it one bit!" Instead, my appropriate self prevails, and I usually ask the client why she called her partner a good man.

I typically hear two responses to that question. The first one is, "Because he really was a good man." Women who say this about men who obviously were *not* good to them tend to fall into one of three categories:

Category 1—Women who have never been treated well by a man or haven't for a long time, and for that reason have a hard time identifying what a good man really is.

Category 2—Women who have been tricked or manipulated into thinking that the way they were treated wasn't so bad.

Category 3—Women who can't or choose not to face the reality of what their partner put them through.

The second response I hear is, "I felt bad about the way I was describing him." Women who say this believe that any time they point the finger of blame at their partner or describe his weaknesses, they are being too critical or unfair. For these women, simply admitting that their partner made mistakes is hard and can cause them to feel like they are bashing him. Some of these women also express a deep sense of responsibility for what they went through with their Ex.

One of the only ways to combat these feelings is to be able to give an honest appraisal of your Ex. If we cannot admit to ourselves and supportive family or friends what happened, we are at risk of forgetting, denying, or minimizing the truth. We may even rewrite the history of the relationship and convince ourselves that it wasn't so bad. You know what that can lead to: going back to your Ex. If every time you talk about your Ex's negative qualities or behaviors you find yourself feeling guilty, sorry for him, or overwhelmed by emotion, take a second to think about why you have those feelings and what is at their root. Is it fear, sadness, grief, anger, loss? In time this self-exploration can lead you to find comfort in honestly discussing with others what you went through without feeling like you need to defend your Ex.

In the end, it doesn't matter if you call your Ex a good man, a bad man, or something else. That is not the point. The point is for you to eventually face the truth about who he was and how he treated you, and then use that awareness to shore up your resolve to resist going back to him.

5

Setting Yourself Up for Success

I took a self-defense course not too long ago. (It was a great course, offered through IMPACT Personal Safety, listed in the Resources.) I was surprised to hear in the first session that about 10 percent of the people in my class (all women) weren't sure if they could make themselves fight another human being—even if they were being attacked! Most people, including me, want to avoid a physical fight, but I'm real clear that if it came down to me or the other person walking away from an encounter they started, then *it's on.*

By the end of the self-defense course, all of my classmates had that same confidence. That's what this chapter is about: reminding you that you are worth fighting for. It provides ten concrete X-ing strategies for effectively karate-chopping your Ex out of your life for good. You are in no way helpless against his attempts to lure or force you to go back to him. By the time you finish this chapter, you will have a black belt in busting your Ex's playbook strategies. You will know that if it comes down to him or you, you won't hesitate to pick yourself.

Mum's the Word

I have spoken to a lot of women who just want to tell their Exes "one more thing." It might be something they think will help the Ex ("I did love you"), something they need to get off their chest ("You were such a jerk to me"), something practical ("I need to come get my TV"), or something to try to set the record straight ("I really never cheated on you").

That one last thing could take the form of a million different words that seem to linger unsaid. The problem with actually doing it—telling him "one more thing"—is that it encourages your Ex to think that you are in some way still interested in having a connection with him. As you will see from the examples below, you could be downright nasty to him, and yet what he takes away from your conversation might be something totally different from what you wanted to communicate. *In the end, it doesn't matter what you intended to tell him; it is what he hears in your words that will get you in trouble.*

Below is a list of communication traps that your Ex may set, how you might fall into them, and what your Ex will think when you do.

Trap #1: Your Ex calls, texts, or e-mails you 101 times.
How you fall in: He has called you 100 times and you've resisted picking up the phone every single time even though it is driving you crazy. On the 101st time you pick up the phone only to tell him *never* to call again. Then you hang up.
What he thinks: Okay, I need to call 100 times before she will talk to me. I better start calling again.

Trap #2: He sends you a really mean e-mail blaming you for everything and blatantly lying about things that mean a lot to you.
How you fall in: You are furious about the e-mail. Before you can

even think about it, you fire off a reply letting him know what you think about him and his lies.

What he thinks: She is still thinking about me. She will respond if I make her mad enough. How else can I fire her up?

Trap #3: He leaves you a bunch of sad voice messages about how he doesn't understand why you left him and how terrible it feels to be without you. He pleads for you to pick up the phone and just talk to him.

How you fall in: You are trying to be nice so you pick up the phone just to tell him again why you cannot be with him. He refuses to hear you, and so you are on the phone for a half hour explaining the same thing over and over before you finally get frustrated and have to hang up.

What he thinks: She feels guilty for what she has done. She still loves me. If I make a big enough deal about how hurt I am, she will come back.

Trap #4: He gets a mutual friend to tell you that he wants to come by to pick up some of his stuff.

How you fall in: You call him, but only to arrange for him to get his stuff.

What he thinks: Great! Now I am finally talking to her. I am going to convince her to let me come over to her house. Then I will be able to see her face to face and talk some sense into her or get some romance going. She won't be able to hold out once I put some moves on her.

I think you probably see the trend here. He does something obnoxious to get your attention. Not knowing any better, you give him some. He takes this to mean that there is still a chance for you to be together and redoubles his efforts. This is a crazy cycle that you do not want to be a part of. Don't fool yourself into thinking that with the right words you will help him understand your decision. There are *no* right words in this situation. He may *never* agree with what you have done. And guess what? He doesn't have to. *You do not need his permission or acceptance to move on with your life.*

Don't Be There

Let me start by saying that this next defensive maneuver is not fair to you. It requires that you rearrange your life even though you are the one who has been treated badly. But if you really want to stay gone from him, you need to make yourself hard to find. This can mean changing your cell phone number, your e-mail address, and maybe even your physical address.

All this may seem like a lot to even think about doing. And it is. But the stakes are very high when it comes to restricting your Ex's access to you. If you are always dodging calls or interactions with your Ex, you will find it very hard to maintain your calm, continue to heal, and find new and exciting people and activities with which to fill your life. One of the nicest things you can do for yourself is to give yourself the space you need to move forward.

Another strategy to consider is changing your schedule. If your Ex knows you go to a certain church every Sunday or to the same grocery store every Thursday night, might he try to meet you at one of those places? Under normal conditions he might not. But if you are not taking his calls or e-mails, be aware that he could use his knowledge of your schedule to intercept you. If you think this may happen, or if it has already happened, whenever possible try to vary your schedule to keep from having any unwanted contact with him.

One client I worked with, Andrea, went to the same bar with her friends from work once a month. After her breakup from Luke, guess who was having drinks at the bar the night she and her friends went? As might be expected, Luke made a scene, and Andrea wound up feeling embarrassed and hurt. Luke ambushing Andrea at the bar was certainly not Andrea's fault, but it might have been prevented had she and her friends decided to go to a different bar (which after this encounter they did). Alternatively, just being aware that Luke might be at the bar could have helped Andrea not be so surprised by his presence. If she didn't want to leave the bar that evening, she might have also been able to formulate a plan in advance for what to do if he confronted her (i.e., let the manager know, give Luke the silent treatment, sit next to one of her big guy friends, make sure to get an escort to her car).

Know, too, that in extreme cases your Ex's persistence can cross the line and turn into stalking. If you have any fear of him or believe he might be stalking you, you should contact the police and your local domestic violence service provider to create a plan for your safety. Stalking is illegal. Too many women endure being stalked because they don't know their rights, they doubt people will take their problem seriously, or they don't know what to do about it.

Shut Down Friends with Messages

You have probably heard of "friends with benefits." That is not at all what I am talking about here. I am referring to those oh-so "helpful" friends, family members, and acquaintances who "want you two to get back together." They may mean well, but boy can they cause a lot of trouble for you. These people very often haven't heard the whole story, and they can't believe your Ex is the person you know him to be.

Commonly, both of you will know someone who feels sorry for your Ex, takes his side, and delivers messages from him to you. Whenever possible you should keep this person at a distance. You may even need to discontinue your relationship with them. Don't be afraid to tell this person very clearly that you do not want to hear from your Ex. You are not being rude. You are simply protecting yourself and setting an appropriate boundary. You might also suggest they read the Appendix at the back of the book. It was created specifically to help friends and family know how best to support you during this difficult time. (This Appendix can also help you to know what the people who love you may be going through in their attempts to be there for you.)

If the person continues to pressure you to talk about or to your Ex, they are disrespecting you and are clearly more concerned with your Ex's wishes than yours. You must ask yourself, "Is this really the kind of person I want around me, now or ever?"

Technology Tip

Think about whether you have any mutual friends or family members who have access to your online activity and may be passing information to your Ex. These could be individuals whom you have "friended" on Facebook, who receive your Twitter feeds, or who belong to the same chat groups or other online communities that you do. If so, consider carefully whether they are sympathetic to your Ex or are vulnerable to being manipulated by him. If you have concern about someone abusing your trust in this way, you may need to have a conversation with them about your worries, block them from your sites, and think seriously about how close you want to be with them.

Forgive Yourself

If you feel bad about things you did during your relationship with your Ex, or if you still have lingering thoughts that you could have done more to fix things, those feelings will be exploited by your Ex. The truth is we can always find ways in which we weren't the perfect partner. You may be bossy, have insecurities, or have a pretty rockin' temper. None of us is perfect. And many good-intentioned, strong-willed women will see the fact that they are still breathing as evidence that they could have tried harder in their relationship. To be sure they were not the problem, they may believe they should go back and put some more of themselves into trying to figure things out with their Ex. But just like with alcohol, you have to know when to say when.

Knowing when to pull the plug is not a bad thing. Just the opposite—it is a skill and a self-protective necessity. In this way, a breakup may be one of your greatest successes. Give yourself credit for recognizing that things were not as they should have been and for leaving. It takes courage to do what you have done. Too often we see leaving a relationship as a failure or a lack of effort or commitment on our part. But if we follow this reasoning to its logical conclusion that would mean we would all still be with our first boyfriend, and I for one would not like that.

Tragically, for many women, leaving a partner seems to be a double-edged sword. We blame ourselves for not trying hard enough to make it work or rake ourselves over the coals for staying as long as we did. Sometimes we torment ourselves with one judgment one day and the other the next! Neither of these unfair attempts to hold ourselves accountable is particularly helpful or productive, and neither takes into account that we were basically learning on the job with our Ex. These judgments just make us feel bad for our decisions. Instead, cut yourself some slack and recognize the positive in what you were trying to accomplish.

In fact, there is no "perfect" amount of love, time, and energy to devote to a person. No line that separates going over-board from quitting too soon. The reason we don't have an agreed-upon standard for judging whether to stay or go is be-cause relationships are messy, complex, and unique to the people in them. Despite relationships' incredible impact on our lives, we aren't taught about them in school or given an in-struction manual. Family and friends may offer some decent encouragement to us on one occasion and on another say just the wrong thing. (As suggested in the last section, if you have family members or friends who want to support you during this difficult time, have them read the Appendix to this book. It will help them be strong allies and stay away from some of the biggest mistakes they might unknowingly make.)

How you handled your breakup or came to the decision to leave may not have been perfect—how could it have been?—but *it is what needed to happen for you.* In retrospect you may wish you had made different decisions, but for now try to focus on the fact that you have a great opportunity to run your life in the way you want, and spare yourself the criticism you or your partner may have heaped on you in the past.

Remind yourself that when you question your decision to leave or focus on things you did wrong, you do much of your Ex's dirty work for him. For example, if your Ex is trying to get you to buy one of the lies described in the section "I Can Change" (Chapter 2), he will find it much easier to make you believe him if you are already suffering from self-doubt or guilt. If you believe, say, that you could have been more patient with him, he might employ Lie #5, "You Can Change and That Will Change Me." He may say, "You know, if you would just be more patient with me, I wouldn't get so upset and we could be happy together." This lie would be ineffective if you didn't al-ready wonder whether his criticism might be true. But because you do question whether patience is a weakness of yours, his use of this lie may deepen your self-doubt and send you back to a bad situation.

The need to forgive yourself for your shortcomings can also arise when you come to realize some of the deeper dynamics of your relationship and your part in them. It is very common after a relationship ends to review what the heck went wrong. The instinct to unravel the good, the bad, and the truly ugly can be really beneficial and therapeutic. After all, you don't want to have the same things go wrong in your next relationship. But don't let what you learn from this process send you back to the old relationship for more.

Maybe you recognize the following pattern: When your Ex had a bad day at work he would come home in a grumpy mood, you would get defensive with him, and eventually he would blow up at you. Once you make this discovery about your part in the dynamic, don't feel you must (a) communicate this to your Ex, or (b) go back to the relationship and try to fix it.

Understanding your past relationship on a deeper level and seeing how things escalated between you two or how you could have behaved better can be fascinating and give you good insight for your next relationship. But don't make the mistake of using your new awareness to try to resuscitate the old dysfunctional one.

Take Your Own Advice

If you have been telling him to lay off the booze, get professional help, or turn to his faith for guidance, then maybe you, too, should be willing to stay sober, get a counselor, or find some spiritual support. I don't mean to be hard on you (God knows you've probably had enough of that). My point is that sometimes it can be easier to diagnose the person we are with than to look at ourselves.

Admitting that you need support is not a bad thing. It is actually a sign that you know yourself and what you can tolerate when faced with stressful circumstances. I nearly always recommend some sort of individual or group counseling for folks trying to stay free from an Ex. Good therapy can be one of the most important tools you can use to help you get and stay strong. Many communities offer resources for low-cost or free counseling.

Other activities that can promote a sense of well-being include yoga, meditation, a spiritual practice, regular exercise, or belonging to a social group. You do not have to be an expert or even engage in these activities daily to get some benefit from them. But do be open-minded about trying something new. The difficult times you are going through may necessitate solutions you haven't considered before.

Technology Tip

You should be forewarned that your Ex may be seeking advice as well. Many websites, and even some books, are dedicated to helping people get their Exes back. Some of the information they provide is both fascinating and slightly horrifying. Within the world of these websites, know that you are the prey and your Ex is the hunter. Here are some of the claims they make:

1. "There's usually a window when your Ex is giving you a chance to make things right. But you need to read the cues to know when this window is, when it isn't, and how to respond the way they're hoping you will." (www .datingadvicesecrets.com/men/10-mistakes-with-ex -lover-b. Accessed June 2012.)

2. "Discover Dirty Psychological Tricks to Quickly & Easily Win an Ex Back After a Breakup" (http://getexback .stoppingbreakup.com/get-ex-back/make-your-ex

(cont'd.)

Technology Tip (cont'd.)

-want-you-back-discover-the-dirty-psychological
-trick-which-will-entice-your-ex. Accessed June 2012.)

3. "Re-attracting your Ex partner is not exactly the same
as attracting someone new. If you want to get your Ex's
interest, you need to show him or her that you have
been making some progress and have changed since the
breakup." (http://www.getexback.net. Accessed June
2012.)

4. "You'll have your Ex begging for your love again!"
(http://www.exboyfriendguru.com/?hop=wizfacts.
Accessed June 2012.)

5. "Put a leash on your partner's heart and pull them back
in before it's too late." (http://www.datingadvice
secrets.com/men/10-mistakes-with-ex-lover-b.
Accessed June 2012.)

6. "Psychological tricks worked! 'Magic of Making Up'
also describes clever psychological tricks for how to get
your Ex back you can use to create instant connections
with your former lover, even if they are adverse [sic] to
reconciliation." (http://www.exbackhelp.biz. Accessed
June 2012.)

Notice that these websites don't give a rat's behind
about you. They don't care what you want or what will
make you happy. Despite the fact that some of them are
operated by licensed psychologists, they don't get into
such complex ideas as whether reuniting is a good thing,
or how hard you may have struggled to stay away from
your Ex. Instead, they're focused on persuasion and tricks.
Some Exes know more about psychological warfare than
the CIA. To think that there are numerous resources online
to help them is beyond disturbing.

Mourn the Loss of the Salesman

If your Ex had consistently been the great guy that he is pretending to be now, or that he was in the beginning, your life with him would have been amazing. Acknowledging that you loved parts of your Ex can help you separate who he is overall from who he is when he's trying to win your heart.

The sad truth is that your Ex is a salesman—and an effective one. As good a judge of character as you may be, he probably sold you early on a buffed and polished version of himself. As we discussed in the last chapter, his aim now is to resurrect your feelings for this nonexistent person. But know that your Ex will not maintain his good behavior or be the man he should be for the long term.

Give yourself permission to mourn the fact that your Ex turned out to be different from who you thought he was. It may feel like grieving the death of someone you love. In a certain way, that's exactly what you're doing. The man you first came to know and care for no longer exists, and that is really sad. Do not blame yourself for failing to see him for what he was from the beginning. We have all been tricked by salesmen who put on a show to get us to believe their promises, only to find out later that we were scammed. Making peace with this injustice will help you move on.

You likely had deep, genuine feelings for who you thought this man to be. Now that you know he isn't that person, you probably will have a lot of pain to work through. It can take time. You cannot let the sadness overwhelm you, and don't let it lead you to make excuses for him, or hope that this time he will be different, or believe that he will keep his promises. To be blunt, the artificial person you fell in love with is gone; he never really existed. Bury him and mourn him. Know that there are men out there who can be as good to you on the 200th date as they were on the first date. That kind of man will see your value without your having to break up with him.

Keep Your Eyes on the Prize

Do you know any couples or single people who are really happy and whose lives you respect and admire? Everyone has hard times, and no one goes through life smiling all the time, but there are plenty of people out there who are satisfied with their lives. While you're coming out of a bad relationship, it can be important to spend time thinking about—and maybe spending time with—individuals who have essentially accomplished what you are setting out to do. *If they can do it, you can too.* In your dark moments you may doubt that you will ever have the life you are seeking. You may wonder if hanging in there is worth the pain and hardship you're going through. Keeping your eyes on the prize by remembering folks you know who are happy can be comforting and inspiring, and it can give you something to work toward.

A related technique is to spend time reliving truly joyful moments from your own life. Really immerse yourself in the memory and let yourself re-feel the good feelings of who you were and still are. Or maybe you have never experienced the sense of well-being and security that you hope to find. If that's true for you, please keep the faith. Know that it is possible—if sometimes challenging—to reshape your life into a satisfying one.

A third important way to keep your eyes on the prize is to vividly imagine yourself experiencing the life you want. You left your Ex for a reason, whether it was your need for affection, respect, kindness, love, consideration, equality, friendship, sharing, support, safety, or something else. When you have a few quiet minutes to yourself, shut your eyes and imagine being in a satisfying partnership that offers the things you really want. Or imagine yourself being alone and happy, really feeling the joy you hope for. What would your new life be like? How would you feel inside? What characteristics might your new partner have? What are the positive changes you've already experienced since your breakup? The imagination is an incredibly powerful tool. This may sound silly to you, but trust me. Imagining a better life—exploring the possibility in your mind and immersing yourself in the good feelings—is the first step to creating it. Many times you are closer to that life than you can see or imagine.

You may believe that only children and teenagers do this sort of day-dreaming, but healthy adults do, too. The beautiful surprise is that when we mentally step out of our present reality and believe in the possibility of something better, we may be rewarded with a life that is even greater than we can imagine. I really hope this happens to you, and I believe it can. The question is, do you?

Put Your Happiness First

What would it take for you to shift to a "happiness first" perspective in your life? That means making your happiness your top priority—before your work, your responsibilities at home, or your nonemergency commitments to your family.

I know this is a radical notion and one that you might immediately have strong negative feelings about. I can almost hear your doubts. "What if Suzy needs to go to the doctor, or I have to get my car fixed, or I have a deadline at work? I couldn't put my happiness first then!" It's true that you will still need to take Suzy to the doctor and handle your major responsibilities. However, those other things that come up? Duties you might normally take on? Can you imagine letting them go in favor of taking care of yourself?

If you are the kind of woman who is always tending to others' needs, or who prides herself on everything she can get done in a day, this idea may terrify you because it will force you to slow down and focus more on *your* needs. But hear me out, because the advantages of this type of perspective for you are huge right now.

Let me say that most folks, and especially people who have just left a toxic relationship, tend to think that putting their happiness first is a selfish—even reckless—way to live. They fear that if they were to put their needs for feeling good over other priorities, all hell may break loose. They will be terrible mothers, employees, sisters, daughters. They will let everyone down, including themselves. They worry that without absolute vigilance, the mountain of responsibilities they have to their jobs, family, friends, you name it will come toppling down and bury them. I understand this fear.

Let's agree that for everyone, even in the best of times, our life responsibilities require enormous amounts of attention. Some days it seems as if every one of them is screaming to be bumped up to first priority. We can come to feel that we are at their mercy, that we get merely the scraps of whatever is left over at the end of the day.

It is entirely possible that the people who rely on you expect you to put them before other priorities, and especially before you tend to something as seemingly extravagant as your own happiness. You may have a family member who really needs a favor today, a child who needs some cookies baked for school, a dog that could use a walk, a house with a leak in the roof, and an unmopped floor. And now I am telling you to add your happiness to the top of this heap of responsibilities? What am I, some kind of sadist?!

Here's why I am asking you to reorganize your priorities at a time when you may feel least able to do so. A person can only handle so much before they simply shut down and become a spectator, frozen and overwhelmed while life passes them by. You will be particularly susceptible to this occurring while you're under the increased stress of living in your post-breakup world. Frozen and overwhelmed people go back to their Exes much more frequently, usually because they're looking for some help to manage their intense emotions and the demanding world around them. Typically they don't get the solace they seek once they return to the Ex, but it can sure seem like a good idea when a tidal wave of obligations and feelings are crashing around you and you are struggling to keep your head above water.

This is exactly why your happiness must come first for a while. Without it you will be unable to tackle your "must-do's," and you may feel the urge to turn to your Ex for relief and support. Even if you are able to avoid that trap, and instead rely on white-knuckle determination to get through life's demands, it will be at your expense. Pushing yourself to an extreme eventually takes a toll on you, both emotionally and physically, leading to exhaustion, crying, hopelessness, guilt, anxiety, or worse. You may already be feeling the effects of trying to juggle your life without taking time for yourself.

You know how when you are on an airplane and the flight attendants tell you about the safety precautions? They say that if the plane loses cabin pressure, an oxygen mask will drop from the ceiling, and they instruct you to put *your* oxygen mask on *before* you help anyone else with theirs—including children. If you don't get your mask on first, you may be able to help your seatmates for a time, but eventually you will run out of air, leaving you with nothing left to give and vulnerable to injury. A "happiness first" focus is like that. If you are coming out of a tough breakup with a man who didn't treat you particularly well, making it a priority to create a basic amount of happiness for yourself will ensure that you can (a) resist your Ex's temptations to lure you back to him, (b) build on that happiness to create more, and (c) have the internal resources to treat others well.

The truth about happy people is that they are less likely to merely take what they are given or to be drawn back to an unhealthy Ex by emotional blackmail. Happy people make better decisions and have more motivation to continue the path forward. Folks who are depressed, filled with shame and guilt, tired, stressed, or isolated often are willing to accept less than they deserve.

How much of your life's joy was sacrificed to your Ex during your relationship? How much was depleted during the breakup, or has diminished due to the stress of your present reality? You must replenish what you have lost or what has been taken from you. Let's say you had a hundred units of happiness at the start of your relationship with your Ex. Or, if not, let's say that is how much happiness you desire. Take a moment to think about how many units you have now. Ninety? Seventy-five? Perhaps fifty units, or even lower? It is up to you to make up for this deficit. In the same way that the body uses nutrients that must be replenished through a healthy diet and maybe some vitamins, our mental and emotional selves require a certain amount of good feelings to stay strong and healthy.

Restoring your happiness may take time, but only you have the power to create the opportunities to do so. Once you are feeling great again—and once you are beyond any temptation to return to your Ex—you may not need to be so vigilant about putting your happiness first. Until then, think about what it would mean to cultivate deep satisfaction in your life on a daily basis. You don't have to be euphoric every day, and I am sure some days it will be hard to even crack a smile. I know you don't live at Disneyland, and you probably don't have the money to go shopping at Neiman's every day. That's okay, because while those things may be a quick fix, what we are shooting for is something more sustainable and ultimately more meaningful. Here is what it will take:

1. Commit to your happiness on a daily basis. Check in with yourself regularly to create mindfulness about your level of happiness.

2. Allow yourself to be creative about and unashamed of your pursuit of this priority.

3. Set boundaries with others who don't respect or who infringe on your need to be happy.

4. Set aside and plan for time to enjoy yourself.

5. Do the things that make you happy.

If you regularly take these steps you will be much better able to achieve your goal of staying away from your Ex, repairing whatever damage you sustained during the relationship, *and* fulfilling all of your pressing obligations.

Below are some examples of activities you might pursue on any given day to increase your happiness. You will notice that most of the ideas on this list cost little or no money and require very little advance planning. The point is to weave joyful activities into your life regularly. What they say is true: life's simple pleasures really are the best.

• buy a new scarf	• take a nap
• go to a funny movie	• look at the stars
• get a massage	• get a haircut
• take a walk	• wear comfortable shoes
• pet your cat	• let the mopping wait
• buy a latte	• buy some flowers
• go swimming	• eat a cupcake

- savor what you are eating
- read a trashy gossip magazine
- go to a counseling session
- take a quiet moment to reflect
- plan for the fun thing you will do tomorrow
- join a group that engages in a hobby or activity you enjoy
- hang out with folks you like (and not the ones who emotionally drain you)

Being happy seems like something that just happens, but it isn't. It takes forethought, creativity, planning, courage, time, and energy to prioritize happiness and then follow through with action. Your Ex may not have supported this type of behavior. He may even have encouraged you in subtle ways to think more about his wants and desires than about yours, or made you feel indulgent when you focused on yourself. Perhaps your parents didn't model self-care and self-nurturing. Do not let this stop you. Give yourself the strategic advantage of having as much happiness in your life as you can.

One warning: do not confuse stuffing down the pain or masking it with creating true happiness. Right now, just to get by, you may feel strongly inclined to consume large amounts of alcohol, eat a whole cake, or stay in bed all day. We've all been there. I know I am really low when I break out the container of Cherry Garcia ice cream and the big spoon. In such moments, know that those self-destructive temptations are a result of your emotional and perhaps physical depletion. Don't judge yourself for those impulses, but do know that following them would not be in keeping with your plan to thoughtfully and intentionally create more joy. Remind yourself that genuine happiness is both your right *and* a vital part of your plan for staying away from your Ex.

6 *Getting Fit for the Road Ahead*

Whether it is getting lousy drunk and calling your Ex, making excuses for him, failing to listen to your instincts, or letting feelings of loneliness get the best of you, there are lots of ways you can sabotage all your hard work to build a better life. If you want to make smart choices in the aftermath of your breakup, you have to be at the top of your game. You have to think carefully about how you feel, about your motives, and about the likely outcomes of your behaviors. That can be difficult given all the distractions your Ex may put in the way.

You have work to do to make sure you stay strong and supported during this time. You need to be willing to get real about where you may be failing yourself. This kind of self-examination is not for wimps.

Whereas Chapters 4 and 5 were about preventing your Ex from spoiling your chances for independence from him, this chapter examines how you could unknowingly hurt your own efforts to X your Ex. Only you can decide how to get through this tough time. If you make good decisions now, you will be in a much better place emotionally to face the coming days, when up may seem like down and getting back together with your Ex may seem easier than staying away.

Self-Discovery Exercise #6:
X-ing Your Ex Boot Camp

We all do things after a breakup that are dumb or even downright harmful to our goal of staying away from our Ex. We drive by his house, look at old photos, re-read emails he wrote us, and obsess over whether he is dating anyone. Wouldn't it be great to be able to attend some kind of breakup boot camp to get us in shape for what lies ahead? If you think of staying away from a difficult Ex as a battle, there are times when women who have been courageously fighting jump over to their Ex's side of the battlefield for no apparent reason and start mowing down their own troops. That is definitely not a winning strategy. To prevent it from happening to you, you must be able to see that what you are doing is counterproductive so you can stop doing it.

Different women are drawn to different self-destructive actions after their breakups. It can be hard to know what little things might trip you up and why. By completing the self-discovery exercise below you will have a better understanding of where and when you are most likely to be your own worst enemy in your efforts to stay gone from your Ex.

For the following questions, please circle the answer that seems to best fit your feelings about the statement. For any questions to which you answer either "I feel this way a lot" or "I feel this way sometimes," pay special attention to the section of this chapter that is listed at the end of the question.

1. *I have the urge to make excuses for his bad behavior.* ("The Top Ten Mistakes," page 116)

   I feel this way: •a lot   •sometimes   • never

2. *I feel that I should take some responsibility for the things he did wrong.* ("The Top Ten Mistakes," page 116)

   I feel this way: •a lot   •sometimes   • never

3. *I have the impulse to care more about his feelings than about my own.* ("The Top Ten Mistakes," page 116)

   I feel this way: •a lot   •sometimes   • never

4. *Even though I wouldn't want someone I love to have a relationship like this, it still feels like I should.* ("The Top Ten Mistakes," page 116)

   I feel this way: •a lot •sometimes • never

5. *When I start to remember the bad stuff he did, I try to forget it.* ("The Top Ten Mistakes," page 116)

   I feel this way: •a lot •sometimes • never

6. *I have the urge to seek advice from people who I know will tell me to get back together with him.* ("The Top Ten Mistakes," page 116)

   I feel this way: •a lot •sometimes • never

7. *I am putting off getting counseling or asking for the support I need from others.* ("The Top Ten Mistakes," page 116)

   I feel this way: •a lot •sometimes • never

8. *I find myself really focusing on the good parts of my Ex and our relationship.* ("The Top Ten Mistakes," page 116)

   I feel this way: •a lot •sometimes • never

9. *I think that because of my faults, I don't deserve any better than my Ex.* ("The Top Ten Mistakes," page 116)

   I feel this way: •a lot •sometimes • never

10. *I am sad because I feel like my hopes and dreams were shattered when I left my Ex.* ("The Top Ten Mistakes," page 116)

    I feel this way: •a lot •sometimes • never

11. *I really want to know why he did those bad things to me.* ("The One Question That Will Make You Fail," page 123)

    I feel this way: •a lot •sometimes • never

12. *Now that I've been gone from him for a while, I am starting to wonder if maybe I didn't end things too soon.* ("The Risks of Healing," page 125)

    I feel this way: •a lot •sometimes • never

13. *I am afraid that one day I will just pick up the phone and call him, and it will all start up again.* ("Thinking: A Spectator Sport," page 127)

I feel this way: •a lot •sometimes • never

14. *I believe that if he loves me enough, we can work it out.* ("Breaking Up Breakup Myths," page 128)

I feel this way: •a lot •sometimes • never

15. *I am hopeful that this breakup will teach him a lesson.* ("Breaking Up Breakup Myths," page 128)

I feel this way: •a lot •sometimes • never

16. *Sometimes I think that if I have a drink it will make me feel better about the breakup.* ("No Drinking and Dialing," page 137)

I feel this way: •a lot •sometimes • never

17. *Whenever I feel lonely, I start to think maybe I made a mistake by leaving.* ("The 'L-Word': Loneliness," page 140)

I feel this way: •a lot •sometimes • never

The Top Ten Mistakes

Women often do certain things after a breakup that are almost sure to send them back to their Ex. Almost all women do these things to some extent, so don't crucify yourself if you catch yourself in the act. Being informed about these potential hazards and noticing when you are putting yourself in jeopardy will make it much less likely that you trip up. The choices you make every day determine whether you are traveling toward your Ex or away from him. *If you return to your Ex, it will not be out of a moment's weakness but because of a sequence of decisions you made along the way.*

Let's talk about the thoughts, decisions, and actions that can lead you back into your Ex's arms as well as the most common mistakes women make post-breakup. The mistakes listed below represent ways in which you forgive your Ex, forget the truth of your dissatisfaction with him, or take the blame when you shouldn't.

▶ Mistake #1: "Things Weren't *That* Bad"

One way you may do that is by dismissing his bad behavior or making it okay. You make excuses for him by thinking or saying, "It only happened that one time, after he was drinking." Or, "I know he didn't mean to say that." Or, "He said the other women didn't mean anything to him." In essence, you're giving him a "get out of jail free" pass, which only allows him to advance his game against you.

▶ Mistake #2: "I Didn't Act So Great Myself"

Maybe you hold yourself responsible for his misbehavior and believe that you drove him to it. In this scenario, your Ex was just a victim of your craziness and your inability to be the person you think you should be. Most women whom I hear taking an unfair amount of blame for the bad things that happened in the relationship do not see how this sort of thinking sets them up to return to their dysfunctional partner. They think they are being healthy and the bigger person for admitting their faults. Ultimately, however, if you mistakenly identify yourself as the big reason the relationship ended, you don't get a pat on the back or a gold star from the universe. You just get another try at a relationship that won't improve despite your attempts to be perfect.

▶ Mistake #3: "He's Really Hurting"

This one involves putting more stock in his feelings than in yours. By focusing on his pain rather than on your own struggles or needs, you are basically choosing him over yourself. And in this case you definitely need to be in your own corner.

If you are not rooting for yourself and thinking of yourself first, you will be setting yourself up to do what he wants, *not* what will make you happy. Usually this means going back to him—and soon.

▶ Mistake #4: "I Wouldn't Wish Him on My Worst Enemy — but Still…"

Women sometimes end up doing things they would never advise others to do. Think of someone you love—your mom, sister, friend, or cousin. If this person had gone through a tough breakup, would you want her to think, say, or tolerate the things you are thinking, saying, or tolerating? Maybe you repeatedly apologize to your Ex for the breakup, or fail to set boundaries with him, or tell yourself and others that the breakup was entirely your fault, or grovel for his forgiveness, or even agree to return to him. Maybe you suffer silently while he repeatedly lashes out at you, calls you names, takes advantage of you, or belittles you in other ways. If you wouldn't want someone you love to be treated that way, why is it okay for you to be?

▶ Mistake #5: "Bad Times? What Bad Times?"

Some women choose not to remember certain hurtful things their Ex did. I know this sounds ridiculous; how can you choose not to remember? Still, I have seen it many, many times. We all have the ability to ignore information that opposes actions we are tempted to take. When properly motivated, we can go into such a state of denial that we refuse to acknowledge things that are right in front of us, such as the "other women," his drinking, the jobs he couldn't keep, the promises he broke, the temper he wouldn't control, the love he refused to share. We have the power to erase painful memories and pretend those events never happened. And once you convince yourself of that, why wouldn't you go back?

❯ Mistake #6: "Maybe His Mother Can Help Me Figure Out What to Do"

Another way women sabotage themselves is by seeking the advice of people who they know will encourage them to return to their Ex. There are probably some people in your life to whom you didn't reveal the unpleasant stuff about your Ex, or who will always want you to be with him no matter how bad he is. If you seek out those folks to talk to, they will most likely recommend that you work things out with him. They may even be pretty convincing, which makes it seem easy and logical to follow their suggestions. That's just another way of orchestrating your own return to him.

❯ Mistake #7: "I Don't Need No Stinkin' Therapy"

Many women don't take advantage of the help and support that exists for people trying to end destructive or dangerous relationships. If you keep all your feelings a secret, refuse to rely on others, allow yourself to be isolated, fail to seek out relevant information, or wallow in your pain, what do you expect will happen? There might be days soon after the breakup when about the best you can do is get out of bed and feed yourself. But you can't live like that for very long and expect to maintain a clean break from your Ex. Be willing to try some of the suggestions in this book for dealing with your grief, pain, and emotional and physical needs.

❯ Mistake #8: "But He's Such a Good (Fill-in-the-Blank)"

Some women focus on one or more of their Ex's good qualities and soon start to obsess over him. "He was so smart." "He was such a good provider." "He was a good Christian." "The sex was explosive." "He was the very best father." A woman can build up the importance of these desirable characteristics to such a degree that she convinces herself they make up for the bad stuff. And then she may worry that she will never find anyone else who has these qualities in such abundance.

One good friend of mine was dating a cold-fish of a guy who happened to be a scientist. She loved his intellect and the stimulating conversations they would have. Sometimes they would talk for hours about his theories and just nerd-out together. She felt so alive during those times with him but initiated a breakup when it became clear that he cared more about his theories than about her. After the breakup, my friend called me to talk about how much she was missing those exciting conversations she and her Ex used to have. She also was pretty down about being able to find another guy with the brains of the last guy. The one thing that seemed to help relieve this pain was her eventual revelation that, yeah, the last guy seemed smart, but how brilliant could he be if he put equations and the lab before the basic needs of his girlfriend? We decided that although the next guy she dated might not have the same IQ as her Ex, he would also not be such a huge dummy as to ignore her worth.

The truth is you may or may not find a guy who has these same great qualities. But even if you don't—*that's okay*. The next guy may or may not have the same cute quirks, be as great in bed, be as funny, make as much money, or be as good looking. But he will likely have other qualities that you value in different—better—combinations. Maybe you will choose someone who is more trustworthy, who is more nurturing, who does what he says he will, who shows you the respect you deserve, who is loyal and good to you, who you have fun with, and who you can be yourself around. Wouldn't some combination of those attributes make you feel like you traded up? The goal is either to be happy on your own or to find a better partner whose presence and love truly improve your life. The bottom line is your Ex didn't.

▶ Mistake #9: "There Goes My Last Hope of Ever Being with Someone"

Idolizing certain of your Ex's traits can lead to an overemphasis on the hopes, dreams, and plans you had with him. I've talked to many women post-breakup who were most hurt by the idea that their plans for marriage, children, financial or emotional security, or companionship were now over. You can ease much of this pain by reframing your understanding of what your breakup means for your future. It is wrong to think that just because you are not with your Ex you have to give up on your deepest wishes. Quite the contrary. Your hopes for the future are bigger than one relationship. You take your desires with you wherever you go. Now you truly are free to pursue your goals, either on your own or with another, more suitable partner.

▶ Mistake #10: "I'm No Prize"

Do you have a habit of downplaying your good qualities? When you criticize yourself and tell yourself you aren't so great, it can make your unworthy partner seem like a good deal. After all, if you are too fat, too hot-headed, not smart enough, or not a good enough partner, then it seems reasonable that you deserve to be with a man who is disrespectful or insensitive. *How you feel about yourself can be a good predictor of whether you can successfully end a bad relationship.*

Self-Discovery Exercise #7: Out with the Bad, In with the Good

To break the habit of negative thoughts, you will need to retrain your brain. When you realize a negative thought has popped into your head, take note of it and gently push it aside. Notice I said the word "gently." Do not judge yourself or create even more negative thoughts. Tell yourself something like, "Oh, there I go again," "No big deal," or "Here's another opportunity for me to retrain myself." Now replace the bad thing you were thinking with a positive message that includes at least one characteristic about yourself that you like. What this might sound like is, "I am too good of a friend and mother to think these awful things about myself." In this way you are talking back to the negative messages and replacing the destructive thought with a self-esteem-building one. But to do this you will need to identify as many characteristics about yourself that you like as possible. Really dig in and think about this. Do you like your sense of humor, loyalty, pretty hair, courage, big heart, intelligence, honesty, or some other quality or skill? Make a list of at least five positive traits you have below. If you feel inspired, just keep on listing good qualities!

1. _____

2. _____

3. _____

4. _____

5. _____

Another solution for negative thoughts is to fight fire with fire. If there are negative thoughts in your head, go spend time with and listen to people who care about you. What do they say about you? Probably some pretty great stuff. When they compliment you do you take time to really feel the compliment or just brush it aside? I've known women who will argue about the compliments people give them. For example, if you try to tell them that they are terrific, they say, "No, I'm not." Imagine what it would feel like to have someone tell you are terrific and to really let that settle into your bones. It feels damn good. So just remember to let it.

Finally, don't sabotage yourself by forgetting the good possibilities you opened yourself up to when you left your Ex. Give yourself some credit: It takes a strong woman to end a relationship and stay away. Congratulate yourself on the opportunities you are creating for yourself. You may not see all of them right now, but over time they will reveal themselves to you. If you focus only on how crappy it feels to be gone from your Ex, your decision to leave him may seem foolish, when in reality it could be the best thing you have ever done for yourself.

The One Question That Will Make You Fail

"Why did he do those things to me?" This is a question asked by every woman in your situation. In my opinion, after all you have been through, you darn well deserve to know the answer. But you never will. Not fully. And the sooner you get over this injustice, the better off you will be.

Anytime someone we love treats us in a disrespectful way, we naturally want to know why. We can become very focused on this question, especially if we are still hurting. Our brain may tell us that if we could just figure out why our Ex did what he did, we could either fix the problem or at least keep it from happening again. It can seem like the ultimate comfort would be to know what was behind it all.

Despite these very real motivations, please do not let yourself get into the rut of repeatedly asking yourself why your Ex did what he did. Eventually you will come up with an answer, when in fact *there is no good answer* for why he put you through so much pain. No matter what theories you, your friends, or your family come up with, all of them are potentially dangerous. By attempting to answer this question you are making an effort to pinpoint what went wrong—what went wrong with him, what went wrong with you, what went wrong with you two as a couple. And once you settle on a reason, if any part of you hasn't moved on from the relationship, believe me, you will be tempted to go back to try to fix it.

Some of the most common reasons women come up with for the failure of the relationship are addressed in other chapters of this book. Everything from his bad childhood to your inadequacies can sound like plausible answers. *Going down that road is a dead end. Your job is not to figure out why he did you wrong, but to make sure it never happens again.* Focusing on the reasons for his bad behavior often leads women to take too much responsibility for what happened, to make excuses for what he did, or to decide that they could do things differently with him in the future. In effect, by obsessing over the "whys" of our past, we can be drawn back in to trying to right the same old wrongs.

Here's a revolutionary idea that will save you much time and heartache: instead of making yourself crazy wondering why he treated you badly, just accept the fact that he did.

Take a second to sit with that advice.

What would it mean for you to accept that he did things he shouldn't have—things you didn't deserve and that were not okay with you? What would it be like to take the attitude that you can no longer be troubled by the unanswerable questions from your past? Be done with them. You put that crazy business to rest when you left him. Do not keep revisiting it. Make your peace with it, and move on.

What I am proposing can be difficult, but remember that you are ultimately in control of your thoughts, not a hostage to them. When you find yourself wondering yet again why he did this to you, gently redirect your thinking to something more productive, like planning some enjoyable activities (see "Put Your Happiness First," in Chapter 5). Remind yourself that in the grand scheme of things it doesn't matter why he did it. This is not a riddle that can be solved. It is what it is, and by trying to unravel it you only give it more power.

The good news is that, over time, the answer to why your Ex did what he did will become less important to you. Usually this happens about the time when you really start to get over him. Interestingly, once you get over him you won't care why he behaved badly. It becomes irrelevant. It is only when you are still emotionally connected to and still have some feelings for your Ex that you search for answers.

The more you can do to heal and to separate yourself from your Ex, the more quickly you will reach the point of not giving a flip why he thinks certain things about you, treated you the way he did, or leads his life the way he does. Those questions will be his problem and never again yours.

The Risks of Healing

Healing is a very good thing, and you deserve it. But sometimes as a person begins to heal, her mind will play tricks on her. Days, weeks, or months after the breakup she may start thinking, "Was it really that bad?" "Maybe I was being too hard on him." "I feel so good now, maybe we can give it another shot." You must remember that you left your Ex for a reason—maybe several reasons. Just because the pain may have dulled does not mean those reasons aren't still valid or are in any way resolved. *Trust that the you who broke up with your Ex knew what she was doing.*

Our brains are wired to make sense of things, to forgive, and to return our bodies to a state of calm after traumatic events. This amazing resiliency lets us reapproach situations that previously may have seemed impossible, and helps us recover after we have been through painful or even dangerous experiences. It helps us reach balance in an unpredictable world. You are programmed to start feeling better at some point after a trying ordeal. Don't confuse this process with a likelihood of repairing your relationship with your Ex or assume it signals a readiness in you to try again with him. These are easy mistakes to make.

When suicidal people start to feel a little better, statistics show that is often when they get the energy to follow through with their plans to end their lives. The same is often true of a person who decides to go back to a dysfunctional Ex. When her body and mind start to repair themselves, even though she feels better—or perhaps *because* she feels better—she is reinvigorated to tackle the same problem that caused her so much distress to begin with.

It's sobering to think that your healing could lead to your undoing. How do you neutralize this risk? Here's how: make it a point to appreciate your ability to bounce back for what it is—another chance to live the life you were meant for. It is a respite from what you have been through, a road map to happiness, a signal that your body and mind are relieved to be in a better situation. You are on the right track, so use any good feelings to shore yourself up for when painful emotions like loneliness, uncertainty, sadness, or loss crop up. That is one of the purposes of states of mind such as happiness, inner peace, joy, and contentment. Don't waste those positive emotions on thoughts of reuniting with your Ex; save them to tap into during moments of grief so you can stay strong when you might be vulnerable to his ploys to get you back.

In these early days post-breakup, it is crucial for you to maintain faith in yourself and preserve your emotional and physical energy. When you're feeling good, don't speculate about what-if scenarios, rationalize your Ex's behavior, or convince yourself that you're finally strong enough to make it work with him. For true healing to occur, you must be smart right now. Avoid wasting time repairing a relationship that deep down you know is doomed.

Thinking: A Spectator Sport

What are you thinking about right now? Besides the concentration required to read this book, your mind may be crowded with thoughts, feelings, and ideas swirling around just below the surface. With all this activity, the brain can go into overdrive, especially when you are going through a tough time or have to make difficult, life-changing decisions. Conflicting thoughts can compete for your attention, leading you to feel confused and overwhelmed and maybe even causing you to do things you later regret.

Of course, none of us act on everything we think. Even if we have a million thoughts a day, we pick only a handful to do something about. That selective ability is great. You certainly don't want to act on every impulsive thought that crosses your mind, especially at this time in your life. How lucky you are to have the ability to figure out *why* you are feeling or thinking something. To do this you need to be interested in your thoughts and feelings. Observe them as they come to you, and be willing to question them and be curious about what triggered them.

Say one day you are feeling lonely and miss your Ex. Take a step back and ask yourself what is at the root of those feelings. Perhaps you miss having someone to talk to, or perhaps you feel like you could use some support. If these are the needs you are having, don't turn away from them or try to pretend they don't exist. That will just cause them to come back stronger than ever. Ask yourself how you can meet them. Yes, you could call your Ex, but what would the consequences be? You'd be opening the door to him in a moment of vulnerability, a potentially dangerous scenario.

If calling your Ex isn't a good idea, what else can you do? If you are asking this question, you have already come a long way. Well done. Now get creative. Who can you tell that you are feeling this way? Can you call a family member or friend for support? Can you love on your pet to get some of those needs for affection met? Can you engage in an activity you enjoy? What about nurturing yourself by taking a bath, or setting an appointment with a counselor who can talk you through your feelings? All of these are options that might help you meet your needs without creating more problems in the future.

This way of dealing with your feelings takes a lot of practice, and no one does it perfectly. *But there is power in knowing that just because you feel like calling your Ex, screaming at him, breaking his stuff, e-mailing him, or inviting him over doesn't mean you* have *to do it.* You can dig deeper, find out what's underneath your feelings and thoughts, and come away with more information about yourself and a plan for getting your needs met. And the truth is, sometimes you are going to have a hard day no matter how much you're working on bettering your life. It is to be expected. Don't let your impulsive thoughts today trigger an impulsive chain of events you'll regret tomorrow.

Breaking Up Breakup Myths

I'm sorry to have to tell you this, but it's not just your Ex you need to outthink; in a way, it is the rest of society, too. There are many widespread beliefs about relationships that unfairly stack the deck against women in your situation. I call them "breakup myths." These deeply ingrained ideas can work to push you back to your Ex, sometimes without your even realizing it. This section will make you aware of these cultural forces so you can see them for what they are. Once the curtain is pulled back, you can choose which beliefs make sense to you and discard those that don't. Choosing to disregard certain common myths will free you from their grasp.

If you learn one thing from this chapter, I hope it is that our culture's breakup myths are not your friends. You may not even know what a breakup myth is, but I bet you believe at least some of them. Why do I think that? Because buying into them is almost inescapable for any American woman, regardless of her race, ethnicity, education level, geographical location, sexuality, or economic status. The problem is that these beliefs can have a strong effect on our behavior, even though many of us have never thought them through. It is important to examine them so you can decide for yourself whether they're true for you. The other thing you need to know about all of the myths listed here is that they work in favor of your Ex, and they can sabotage your efforts to stay away from him.

▶ Myth #1: It Takes Two to Tango, and When a Relationship Ends, It Is Both People's Fault

How This Myth Makes Your Life Difficult
If it is always both people's fault when a relationship ends, than it stands to reason that if you were to fix your end of things maybe the relationship would work. It is tempting to think that if you just try a bit harder things can be different. But you have already tried as hard as you could. Give yourself credit for those efforts, and don't second-guess them. This myth can make you feel guilty and at fault, and you don't deserve that. Your Ex will also probably try to make you feel this way, because if you feel guilty about your decision to leave you are much more likely to go back.

The Truth
As with all good myths or lies, there is a bit of truth in this statement. None of us is perfect; we can always find things we wish we had done differently in our relationships. But does

that mean we share equal fault in a relationship's end? I have two problems with this thinking. First, sometimes the end of a relationship is a really good thing, and in those cases I think a person should be commended for ending it. I suggest you wear your role in the breakup like a badge of honor that reads, "I successfully ended a dead-end relationship that was keeping me from the happiness I deserve!" A second reason this saying is bunk is because I have seen many, many cases in which it was one partner who screwed things up for both people. It is hurtful for the one who has been misused to be convinced they played a role in their own mistreatment.

▶ Myth #2: A Breakup Can Whip a Man into Shape and Teach Him a Lesson

How This Myth Makes Your Life Difficult
I have heard many women give each other this bit of advice without knowing how much damage they're doing. It makes sense in a certain way that if we wield the ultimate threat of leaving, maybe we can get what we always wanted—him to change. If breaking up with him doesn't work, what will? Sadly, nothing you do will change him. This is a painful fact to accept. It is easier to believe that your final act of ending the relationship is just what he needs to get his act together.

The Truth
While it is common for a breakup to make a man realize he wants his Ex back, that is not the same thing as his *changing* into a healthy partner. It may feel good to know that he likes you enough to entice you, but you must carefully consider what he is offering. Things may be sweet for a while after the reunion, but soon the relationship—and he—will settle into the same patterns as before. Is that a good thing for you?

▶ Myth #3: If a Man Fights a Breakup and Tries to Win You Back, It Shows That He Really Loves You or Has Changed, and That You Are Supposed to Be with Him

How This Myth Makes Your Life Difficult

Like John Cusack standing outside his girlfriend's bedroom window with a boom box, if your Ex makes a big romantic gesture or is tenacious in his efforts to get you back, it can create the expectation that you will return to him. He might call you a bunch of times, leave you gifts, tell your family how deeply he cares for you, or come up with creative ways to let you know he still loves you. Whether you feel happy that he finally recognizes your worth or angry that he waited to do so until after you left him, his grand deeds may put pressure on you to believe that you are supposed to be with him. As the myth implies, saying no to a man who professes to love you is mean, selfish, or reckless. There are many women out there looking for a man to love them, and if you just cast one away, you must be crazy!

The Truth

The fact that your Ex may still have feelings for you cannot be enough for you to stay with him—even if you have feelings for him too. Here are the more important questions: Does he consistently treat you well? Does being together make you happy? Is the relationship good for you? Does it help you be the person you want to be? Are you safe emotionally and physically at all times? If the answer to any of these questions is no, then it really doesn't matter how many displays of love he puts on.

▶ Myth #4: You Should Never Leave a "Good Man"

I hear this dangerous myth a lot, and I've dealt with it in depth in the section "Don't Use the 'Good Man' Excuse" (Chapter 4). I highly recommend that you read that material if you haven't already. Bottom line: You can leave whoever you want, and your Ex is not a good man, or he would have treated you better.

▶ Myth #5: It's Okay for a Man to Go to Extremes to Try to Get You Back

How This Myth Makes Your Life Difficult

Many people will encourage you to see your Ex's tactics to get you back as acceptable or romantic. As the saying goes, "All is fair in love and war." When he calls your mom to ask her to tell you to go back to him, or leaves love notes on your car, or texts you friendly messages multiple times a day, very few people will pick up on how coercive his behaviors are. They're more likely to think, "Oh, isn't that sweet." No, it isn't. It's sneaky, manipulative, and messed up. Men are encouraged to continue such behaviors, and you are encouraged to put up with them.

The Truth

This strategy of your Ex's is not okay. He does not get a free pass on a behavior just because he does it to get you back. True, a phone call or a note from an Ex does not make him a monster, but there is a line that should not be crossed, and in your gut you know where it is for you. Some of his attempts aren't cute; they're downright despicable, and they need to be recognized as such. Often, he's not even thinking about what is best for you, just what *he* wants. This is selfish and shows yet again how comfortable he is ignoring your wishes and well-being.

Learn to see manipulative behaviors for what they are, and don't be tempted to excuse your Ex for fighting dirty to get you back. Fighting dirty includes subtle acts that on the surface seem sweet. Sending you a card that says "I'm sorry," and including an old photo of him with your children at the zoo may seem thoughtful, but it's just the sort of ploy used by a dysfunctional Ex to work his way back into your heart.

▶ Myth #6: A Woman Who Doesn't Reward the Efforts of a Man Trying to Win Her Back Is a Bitch

How This Myth Makes Your Life Difficult

This one makes my blood boil. I have seen women inflict this myth on other women by making them feel like their Ex's attempts to get them back are a favor they don't deserve. We girlfriends need to remember that just because we see the red roses he sends or the gifts he gives to the children, we don't know the whole story between our friend and her Ex. When we encourage someone to go back or make her feel bad for not doing so, we could be pushing her into a bad relationship. Many women who have to ignore their partner's repeated manipulations believe they are cold-hearted for not jumping back into his arms.

The Truth

All the gifts, compliments, promises, and romantic deeds in the world cannot erase what he did—or didn't do—when you were together. No matter how much he humbles himself to you now, it does not mean that he has changed or that your relationship will be different. *A man who is good at making up with a woman has often had a lot of practice.* You don't want a man who treats you like you are special only after you have walked out the door. At that point it is too late.

▶ Myth #7: You Owe People a Second Chance

And the corollary to this myth: If you have already given someone a second chance, then you owe him a third chance, and if you have already given him a third chance, then you owe him as many chances as he wants to keep asking for.

How This Myth Makes Your Life Difficult

Women are expected to harbor an unlimited supply of forgiveness, and if they say no to their Ex's request for a second or millionth chance, then they are seen as the defective ones. In my opinion, women in general give *more* chances than they should, not fewer. Most women's decision to leave comes only after deep soul-searching and after having given their partners many opportunities to do things differently. When the Ex begs for "one more chance," usually he's already had a number of them. Relenting when your Ex pushes you to take him back diminishes the power of any boundaries you set with him.

The Truth

This myth doesn't provide any guarantee that things will be different if you return to your Ex. All it does is make you believe it's your responsibility to forgive him even if doing so isn't smart, and that there's something wrong with you if you refuse to forgive him. I don't think I have ever talked to a women coming out of a tough breakup who said she hadn't worked hard on the relationship.

Forgiveness and fresh chances are important. But for *you*, not for him! You've already decided that leaving was your best option. Now is a good time to forgive yourself for whatever you still feel guilty about, and give yourself another chance to find love and happiness. Over time you can forgive your Ex for what he did to you. But if you give someone another chance when you know better, you are not being a generous, kind, forgiving person. There is nothing noble in trading your welfare for his.

▶ Myth #8: If He Is Sad Because of the Breakup and You Go On with Your Life, You Are Being Selfish

How This Myth Makes Your Life Difficult

If you start to feel better after the breakup or just have a good day and want to go out with friends, some people may hold it against you. They may be friends of yours who feel sorry for your Ex, your Ex who hears that you are making it on your own and feels sorry for himself, or even your family members who still like your Ex and want you to get back together with him. Some women even come down on themselves when they start to feel better if they know that their Ex is still struggling with the breakup. Women sometimes think that as long as he feels sad, they should too.

The Truth

This is ridiculous. There is no mourning period that you should observe after a breakup. If anyone deserves to have a good day it is a woman who has had a rough breakup. Appreciate the fact that you're feeling fine, and go out and have a great time. Don't spend one second thinking about your sad Ex. You need to have some fun, and if you spend your time feeling guilty you will find it harder to resist your Ex when he makes a play. Your Ex knows this. He may say, "So you're going out tonight. It must be nice to be able to get over us so soon." Or, "Wow, it sure has been easy for you to move on. I still think about you every day." Statements like these are intended to make you feel like a jerk. Your mutual friends might also get in on the act: "I can't believe you are going on a date. Don't you know Mike is still broken-hearted over you?" Stand your guard against these accusations, and don't let anyone tell you not to have a good time. On days when you feel shaky and weak, you can look back on the fun you had, see that your life isn't all bad, and know that you have more happy times ahead of you.

▶ Myth #9: Love Conquers All

How This Myth Makes Your Life Difficult
When people think that love is all you need to make a relationship work, they're ignoring the other important things: respect, communication, effort, nurturing, and compromise. Those elements aren't a given just because you love a person.

A variation on this belief is that you and your Ex should be together because you still have feelings for each other.

This myth also highlights how people define love in many different ways. In my opinion some people have pretty loose definitions of love. I have heard people say they love each other but then seen them treat each other terribly. Is that really love? I don't think so. Just because I say the sky is orange doesn't make it so. Likewise, just because someone says they love you doesn't make it true. This myth encourages you to ignore your questions about whether your Ex's love for you is enough or even genuine.

The Truth

What a huge amount of pressure to put on love! I mean, love is great, but can it really conquer all? Let's put it to the test. Can my love for my Ex keep him from calling me names, or from withholding affection, or from being selfish? Can it keep us from arguing, make me feel hopeful about our future together, or make him be a better dad? Can it take back everything he did to cause me to lose trust in him? Can it erase my memories of the bad times? The answer is no, it can't. Love can conquer a lot, but you need more than love to overcome obstacles like these.

Many clients I've worked with stay trapped in unhappy relationships due to this myth. They are still in love with their partners, at least a little bit, and harbor hope that their love will eventually turn things around. But holding a trace of love for someone does not mean you should try to hold onto him. Love is tough. It can endure many insults and lots of poor behavior. I have talked to women who have been treated badly for years yet who still say that a piece of themselves loves their partner. I don't tell them, "Well, if you still love him, then you should work it out." Quite the opposite. I usually say, "Even if you love him, that doesn't mean you can or should be together."

❯ Miscellaneous Myths

Here are a few other harmful myths that may block you from feeling good about your decision to move on:

- If you are strong enough, pretty enough, smart enough, and confident enough, he will see the light and change for you. If he hasn't changed, that means you are not enough.

- Standing by your man or sacrificing yourself for the relationship is what good, honorable women do.

- You have only so much time to grieve or be sad about the end of a relationship. After that you just need to get over it.

Who taught us this crap? I can't always put my finger on where I learned these myths. Can you? I may not know where they came from, but I know their dangers. If left unexamined, each of them can prevent you from winning your freedom. Because you may hold these beliefs without realizing it, maybe you feel a pull to go back and don't know why. Buying into these old ideas puts you at a disadvantage if your Ex or someone else wants to use them against you. It's as though you're taking a knife to a gun fight while your Ex is loaded up like Rambo. Now with your new understanding of these myths, you have all the ammo you will need to help you see right through these tired, old clichés.

No Drinking and Dialing

I can sum up this section in seven words: "Don't get drunk and call your Ex!"

Like much of what you've read in this book, you already know this but may need a reminder. If you know you get weepy, angry, sex-crazed, or lonely when you drink, then don't. One of the ways women fall back into old relationships is by convincing themselves they can hold their liquor, or that drinking will be just the outlet they need for their pain, sadness, or anger. Friends tend to be really bad about reinforcing this attitude and encouraging a gal to get drunk after a breakup. Did you know that alcohol is classified as a depressant? You already have a depressant in your life—it's called your Ex. Believe me, you do not need another one.

Let me be clear: I am not against enjoying a girls' night out. It can be fun and feel good to cut loose, especially if you have been so focused on your former relationship that you've grown distant from others or haven't gone out in a while. But way too many otherwise smart, level-headed women end up drunk-dialing their Ex to chew him out, cry about how bad they feel, or beg him to come back. If you have had anything to drink—or to smoke, for that matter—you will be more vulnerable to your Ex's manipulations. If you plan to booze it up a bit, make sure you consider the risk you are running and be as careful as possible. You may want to appoint a wing-woman for the night who will keep an eye on you and your behaviors. But know that if your wing-woman "falls in the bottle," or if you get sneaky about calling your Ex, all bets may be off. As big a bummer as this sounds, it is probably better to save the margaritas for later—after you have healed a bit and have moved on to happier times.

While we're on the topic of alcohol and drugs, if you have any addictions, as a strategy for staying gone from your Ex, you will need to address them. All too commonly, women who have been through difficult relationships turn to alcohol or drugs for comfort and to numb the pain. Any dependence on substances really works against you at this stage. In fact, *if you have recently left a dysfunctional relationship and feel that you may have a problem with chemical abuse, getting and staying sober must be goal number one.*

Women who use are at a much higher risk for being lured back into their old relationships. Their Exes can use their addictions against them in all kinds of creative ways. Maybe he makes you feel guilty about it, blames it for all the problems between the two of you, uses it to make you feel like an unfit mother, degrades you for it, or sabotages your efforts at sobriety. Your Ex may not even want you to stay sober. An addicted woman is a vulnerable woman—one who can be more easily manipulated and controlled. Finally, a substance addiction dramatically impairs your reasoning, self-esteem, and ability to protect yourself from harmful influences, all of which combine to create a dangerous recipe.

I know that adding to your present worries by addressing your dependence on drugs or alcohol can feel like an impossible task. I wish it were possible to put it off until you're feeling stronger, but it doesn't work that way. Do not make the mistake of thinking that your addiction is separate from your relationship issues; the two are usually intertwined.

The good news is that if you can stay gone from your Ex you will have less motivation to use, particularly if your drinking or drugging was influenced by your toxic relationship. On the flip side, if you can keep from using you will be much more likely to stay away from your Ex for good. Addressing either of these issues means you will be working on the other. But the reverse is true, too. If your drinking or drugging is out of control, your judgment—and your ability to keep away from your Ex—will be seriously impaired. And if you decide to return to a dysfunctional relationship, your reliance on your drug of choice will likely intensify.

Successfully leading a drug-, alcohol-, and Ex-free life requires support and vigilance. Please avail yourself of whatever resources you need, whether it's time in rehab, going to counseling, enrolling in an outpatient treatment program, or attending meetings of Alcoholics Anonymous or Narcotics Anonymous. Used in combination with the other suggestions outlined in this book, these strategies will dramatically increase your odds of having the life you deserve.

The same principles apply if you have depression, an anxiety disorder, post-traumatic stress disorder (PTSD), bipolar disorder, borderline personality disorder, an eating disorder, or another mental-health issue. Particularly during the post-breakup period you must pay attention to how you are doing emotionally, *especially* if you have a mental-health diagnosis. Your symptoms may increase for a while, and you may need help managing them through counseling and/or medication. Do not ignore changes in your mood, sleep patterns, eating patterns, energy levels, memory, or any other area of your life. You need to be as emotionally strong and balanced as possible so you can make good decisions. Now is not the time to abandon any of the support systems that help you feel better, such as counseling, medication, or group therapy.

The "L" Word: Loneliness

Loneliness is awful. It can make you feel desperate, hopeless, and pathetic. It may be one of the most persistent painful emotions you experience after a breakup, and it is one of the biggest dangers to you now. If you aren't careful, loneliness can take over, jump in the driver's seat, and compel you to reconnect with your Ex. It's not simply that you miss him. Loneliness can be made even worse because you're facing loss on several levels:

1. You're experiencing a decrease in emotional connection overall, even though the connection with your Ex was destructive or dissatisfying. We all need people to talk to, people who care about us, and people whom we

can nurture and be nurtured by. Now that your Ex is out of your life, naturally you will miss the ways in which he filled those needs. Even if he was mostly neglectful or cold, it was probably still comforting to have someone to come home to after a hard day. *If your life away from your Ex is worse than your life with your Ex, it will be hard to stay away for the long term.*

Your task now is to find other ways to create connections with people. This can be a challenge. You may have fallen out of practice reaching out to your friends. You may even have given up some of your friends while you threw all of your energy into making your relationship work. Or maybe your Ex encouraged you to ignore your friendships. It can be humbling to let others know how much pain you are in or how much you need them now. Women often pride themselves on taking care of others and not needing to be taken care of. Now is not the time for walling yourself off from others. If you want to feel less lonely, you will need others to step in and help. Don't be afraid to ask them. You would do it for someone else, and in the future you may have that chance.

2. You're experiencing a decrease in physical touch and affection. I am not just talking about sex, but also about needing a hug or wanting to hold someone's hand. Human beings have an innate need to be touched. We cannot live without it. Even sleeping next to someone and hearing their breathing can be soothing. A lack of physical affection of all types can trigger loneliness and encourage you to minimize your Ex's bad behavior. Acknowledging that fact is an important step to figuring out what to do about it.

   There are ways to get physical nurturing without sleeping around. Small things like asking someone for a hug can help. Many counselors hug their clients because hugging can be very therapeutic. Of course, there are people from whom asking for a hug isn't appropriate, like your plumber. But you probably have a girlfriend or family members whom you can ask for a hug or another type of touch, like offering to do each other's hair or makeup. You can also schedule a massage or a mani/pedi to get the human touch you need. Petting an animal can be very soothing. I have a friend whose beloved older dog died, and she is not yet ready to get a new dog. She and her husband go to the dog park just to pet and enjoy other people's animals. She says that sometimes she feels silly being there without a dog, but that she just needs the unconditional love which animals are so good at providing.

To ignore these natural needs for nurturing or pretend you don't have them is a dangerous gamble. You can become overwhelmed with emptiness and mistakenly believe that only your Ex can fill it.

3. You may have had to give up friends, loved ones, or hobbies in order to leave your Ex. Usually following a breakup, friends get divvied up or take sides. Pre-breakup, perhaps you belonged to a warm circle of friends, went to a certain place of worship, or participated in a bowling league. Post-breakup, some of those friends may want nothing to do with you, your Ex may have staked his claim at church, or maybe he's convinced the bowling team that you're the villain. Where does that leave you? Friendless, churchless, and teamless. That state of affairs will not work for long. You need friends and healthy interests to shore you up as you weather the emotional storms of this turbulent period.

Self-Discovery Exercise #8:
Have You Become More Isolated?

Make a list of all the people or activities you have been separated from in any way due to your breakup:

1. _____
2. _____
3. _____
4. _____
5. _____

In short, breaking up with your Ex may have isolated you from much of the support you relied on. Don't let feelings of isolation and loneliness push you back into a relationship you don't want. *Remember: "Connection equals protection."* The more connected you are to other people, your hobbies, work, your faith, family, friends, school, you name it, the more protected you are from your Ex's attempts to get you back. Think about it. Who is more likely to return to a bad situation? Someone who is alone, or someone who has a life full of love, interesting pursuits, goals, and perhaps a faith in something larger than herself? I think the answer is pretty obvious.

I understand that you probably don't feel like making new friends or picking up a new hobby right now. Ironically, this is exactly what you need to do. Think about the relationships you may have ignored, and invest your time in strengthening them. The turmoil we feel when we separate from a partner can increase our need for emotional closeness. This is a horrible trick that nature plays on us, but we are able to do something about it. If your Ex is still going to your church, pick another one, read your spiritual text at home, go to a study group, or attend church at a different time. If he took your friends away, make new ones. Do not be the victim of his bad actions.

Instead, find creative ways to work around his attempts to isolate you. You may not have realized it before, but your personal and spiritual connections are important to your happiness. If they disappear, you may attribute your sorrow to the breakup when in fact you just need to build more connections.

Self-Discovery Exercise #9:
How Toxic Is Your Loneliness?

We are all lonely at times, but if you lack certain types of support you will be more vulnerable to this painful emotion. Because feelings of loneliness can be a major factor in determining whether you return to your Ex, you need to know where your strengths and weaknesses lie.

This quiz will help you identify the parts of your social life that you may choose to build up in hopes of soothing your feelings of pain and grief and shortening the time it takes to put your Ex behind you. It can also show you where you already have consistent support.

Please read each question and circle the answer that seems to fit most closely.

How is your:

1. Connection to family?

   • **strong**   • **could be stronger**   • **not very strong/no connection**

2. Connection to friends?

   • **strong**   • **could be stronger**   • **not very strong/no connection**

3. Connection to community (neighbors, ex-neighbors, community activities, volunteer opportunities)?

   • **strong**   • **could be stronger**   • **not very strong/no connection**

4. Connection to spirituality?

   • **strong**   • **could be stronger**   • **not very strong/no connection**

5. Connection to your work?

   • **strong**   • **could be stronger**   • **not very strong/no connection**

6. Connection to coworkers?

 • **strong** • **could be stronger** • **not very strong/no connection**

7. Connection to yourself/self-esteem?

 • **strong** • **could be stronger** • **not very strong/no connection**

8. Connection to a hobby(ies)?

 • **strong** • **could be stronger** • **not very strong/no connection**

If you answered "could be stronger" or "not very strong/no connection" to any of the questions, think about ways in which you could improve those connections. You may need to determine whether that's a good idea in every case. For example, if your family has consistently been a negative influence, then don't feel you must strengthen those ties right now, or if you are an atheist, then strengthening your spirituality will probably not top your list. You get to pick and choose which connections will benefit you and which won't.

If you answered "Strong" to any of the questions, then take a minute to recognize that this is an area where you already have a lot of support. When you are feeling sad or angry or are thinking about doing something that you might regret, rely on these strong connections for comfort and good advice. Staying away from a hurtful Ex isn't something most women can do on their own. We all need people and activities that make us feel better and remind us who we are and why we are worth fighting for.

Conclusion: You're Worth It

I am not going to pretend that leaving a relationship is easy. I know it's not. As I hope this book has demonstrated, I take the challenges involved in leaving your Ex very seriously. So I want to help you prepare as much as possible for some of the difficulties that may lie ahead.

Some women go back to their Exes only because they can't tolerate the pain of staying away. Their decision to return is not based on their love for him or because they've been fooled into thinking he has changed. Any number of factors can wear a woman down. She may grow tired of fending off her Ex's attempts to get her back. Early on, she may be unable to see her life getting better without her Ex. She may feel an acute sense of loneliness. She may worry that she doesn't have what it takes to reach her goal. Or she may believe she doesn't deserve any better. Some or all of these influences can combine to make the early post-breakup period very, very difficult. They can even trigger symptoms such as sleep disturbances (including sleeping more than usual), anxiety and stress, an increase or decrease in appetite, crying spells, and deep feelings of grief and sadness. Your experiences will be specific to you, your situation, how ruthless your Ex is in his attempts to get you back, and how much support you have.

I can't provide a formula to determine when you will feel the relief you are looking for. But I can tell you that *you must walk all the way through the fire to get to the other side.* The path you are on is well trod by many, many women who have done what you are doing now. The pain you feel is like a rite of passage. Every day you endure it brings you closer to healing, happiness, and the opportunity for a better life.

If you have any concerns about the intensity of your feelings, or about any physical or emotional symptoms, please talk to a doctor or counselor. A professional will be able to help you figure out if what you are experiencing necessitates other remedies or indicates a larger issue.

Maybe you're wondering, "What's the point? I hurt when I am with him, and I hurt when I'm not. I might as well go back. At least that is a pain I know." I have heard this sentiment from many women who were frustrated, confused, emotionally raw, or overwhelmed by all they had been through. I don't blame them or you for feeling that way. I completely understand where those feelings come from. Maybe it will help to be reminded of the benefits that await you.

Remember that, over time, you have the opportunity to create a happier, more fulfilling life. Returning to your Ex would destroy that chance at a new start. What you had with your Ex wasn't so good, so why not roll the dice and see if opening a new door can bring you happiness?

Be aware that it may take some time before you can completely evaluate the impact your Ex had on you. I have a family member who was diagnosed with celiac disease, which is a strong intolerance to the gluten contained in wheat flour. She told me that after she stopped eating flour for a week she realized she had basically been living with a stomachache her whole life without even realizing it. Can you imagine that? In the same way, you may not yet recognize how toxic your old relationship was or how living with it affected you. And you may not yet know how great life can be without it. It may be months or even years after your breakup before you are fully aware of all the stomachaches your Ex caused you and what life is like without them. I know it must feel like torture to wait so long for relief, but hanging in there is the only way to create a better life for yourself.

This better life may eventually include a new partner—one who treats you well and gives you the respect you deserve. *Before then*, and even more importantly, you will experience an increasing contentment in being true to yourself and honoring your own dignity as you demonstrate to yourself and others what it means to believe in yourself, to stand up to anyone who would demean or diminish you, and to fight for your dreams. Your sense of satisfaction for your accomplishment will be profound, and you will be the hero of your own life. This country erects statues to soldiers who have defended it, to presidents, and to other great leaders—to people who refused to give up on their visions. I honor you for refusing to give up on yours, and I hope that one day you will grasp the magnitude of your accomplishment in staying away from a bad Ex forever. Until then, remember that only you have the power to X that Ex.

Resources

Self-Empowerment Books and Programs

Beck, Martha. *Finding Your Way in a Wild New World: Reclaim Your True Nature to Create the Life You Want.* New York: Free Press, 2012.

De Becker, Gavin. *The Gift of Fear: Survival Signals That Protect Us from Violence.* New York: Little, Brown, 1997.

IMPACT Personal Safety (Courses teaching verbal and physical skills for healthy boundary setting, and self-defense)
PO Box 931541, Los Angeles CA 90093
(323) IMPACT-8 (467-2288)
www.impactpersonalsafety.com

More Information on Manipulative, Controlling, or Abusive Relationships

Bancroft, Lundy. *Why Does He Do That? Inside the Minds of Angry and Controlling Men.* New York: The Berkley Publishing Group, 2002.

Berry, Dawn. *The Domestic Violence Sourcebook.* New York: McGraw-Hill, 2000.

Jayne, Pamela. *Ditch That Jerk: Dealing with Men who Control and Hurt Women.* Alameda, CA: Hunter House Publishers, 2000.

Katz, Jackson. *The Macho Paradox: Why Some Men Hurt Women and How All Men Can Help.* Naperville, IL: Sourcebooks, Inc. 2006.

Stark, Evan. *Coercive Control: How Men Entrap Women in Personal Life.* New York: Oxford University Press, 2007

For Professionals Working with People Who Have Left Hurtful Relationships

Van Dernoot Lipinsky, Laura. *Trauma Stewardship: An Everyday Guide to Caring for Self While Caring for Others*. San Francisco, CA: Berrett-Koehler Publishers, 2009.

National Agencies and Hotlines That Assist with Questions on Abuse

The Childhelp National Child Abuse Hotline
(800) 4-A-CHILD (800-422-4453)

Futures Without Violence
100 Montgomery St., The Presidio
San Francisco CA 94129
(415) 678-5500   Fax: (415) 529-2930   TTY: (800) 595-4889
www.futureswithoutviolence.org

National Coalition Against Domestic Violence
One Broadway, Ste. B210
Denver CO 80203
(303) 839-1852   Fax: (303) 831-9251   TTY: (303) 839-8459
E-mail: mainoffice@ncadv.org
www.ncadv.org

National Domestic Violence Hotline
(800) 799-SAFE (7233)   TTY: (800) 787-3224

National Network to End Domestic Violence (NNEDV)
2001 S Street NW, Ste. 400
Washington DC 20009
(202) 543-5566   Fax: (202) 543-5626
http://nnedv.org/contact.html

Appendix
For Friends and Family Members Who Want to Help

When thinking about who gets hurt by destructive relationships, we may forget about the woman's friends and family members, who have witnessed and in many ways endured the painful realities of the relationship and of its sometimes torturous end. Supporting a friend or relative through leaving a bad Ex is not for the faint of heart. It can be a twenty-four-hour-a-day, seven-day-a-week, gut-wrenching job that is sure to tax your patience, empathy, and powers of self-control. The frustration, sadness, worry, and anger you may feel during this time can be overwhelming, yet you are called on to selflessly set aside your own pain so you can continue to be a rock for your even more embattled loved one.

Friends and family members give an amazing gift of support to women who are leaving hurtful Exes. These caring people often hear the painful details of how their loved one continues to be hurt by her Ex, struggles to sever ties with him, is tempted to return to him, grapples with her own insecurities and doubts—and the impact all of this has on the children. And yet, even though friends and relatives experience the play-by-play and exquisite pain of the leaving process, they have a very limited authority to do anything about it. After all, *you* can't keep your loved one's Ex from playing dirty tricks to get her back, or prevent her from returning to him in an impulsive moment. In many ways, friends and family members are hostage to what is happening around them. They must ride this emotional rollercoaster with little or no ability to get off of it.

You're in an unenviable position. In fact, it sucks. It can make you feel out of control, sad, angry, and fearful, which in turn can make you lash out at your loved one in an attempt to finally end her suffering (and yours). This is when I see people who truly want to support their loved one unintentionally doing the opposite. It happens when friends and family members lay down ultimatums, take shots at the woman's self-esteem, or stand in judgment of her decisions. Behaviors such as these are definitely to be avoided, but during emotionally charged times they may seem like your last resort.

Not all support from friends and relatives is equally valuable. Some ways of helping can afford more positive results for both the helper and the helpee than others. This Appendix describes the three biggest mistakes I observe on the part of friends and family members of women who are leaving destructive or dangerous relationships. Each mistake is followed by concrete advice that will aid you in being her rock during these trying times, instead of inadvertently being a stumbling block in her path.

I so appreciate and respect the people who endeavor to help women leave partners who treat them poorly. It is my sincere hope that the following information will assist supportive friends and family in their noble and worthy cause. In case you haven't heard it recently, you are our heroes, and your influence makes a difference in this world. Please remember that regardless of what choices your loved one makes, no true act of kindness from one human being to another is ever wasted.

Mistake #1: Being a Know-It-All

Goes something like this: "She's crazy! I tell her exactly what to do about her Ex, but she just won't listen to me."

If you are reading this book, you probably have begun to understand the importance of staying away from this kind of only-I-know-best thinking. You have recognized that perhaps there is more to what your loved one is going through than first meets the eye, and that as much as you may know about breakups and life, there is more to learn. You may also now be hip to the fact that in the midst of the emotional tug-of-war your loved one is going through, you can only, in the best of cases, assert so much influence over her decisions. You may get to make lots of decisions in this life, but whether your loved one stays away from or returns to an unhealthy Ex is up to her. Even though it is difficult to witness her being hurt and perhaps making mistakes, she is ultimately the expert on her life and the one who must live with her decisions. Know that if you don't agree with the choices she makes you can still gently plant seeds about different options and at the same time continue to bolster her belief in herself. Over time, and in conjunction with other positive messages and experiences, the seeds you plant may help her make good decisions—ones that lead to her health, safety, and happiness.

Hopefully you have also noticed that any use of time-worn favorites like, "He's just a loser," "What's wrong with you, why can't you just move on," or "You must be crazy to put up with that" are destined to backfire and make you the bad guy. This is because attacking the sanity or good sense of a person who is struggling to break free of a bad Ex is the reverse of what is actually helpful. These phrases cut her down at a time when she is already doubting herself and possibly feeling unworthy and alienated. This is not a good strategy if you hope to help her make healthy, empowered decisions.

Instead of believing that you know best how to run her life, try the following strategies for bringing your A-game to the task of supporting her.

▶ Educate Yourself

In situations where the stakes are incredibly high, it is useful to rely on more than just your good intentions to guide you. An educated helper is a more effective helper. If you haven't yet done so, I highly recommend reading the rest of this book and utilizing the list of resources to aid you in gaining more insight about what your loved one is going through and in responding appropriately. You may also want to offer this book to the person you are trying to help, let them know about the book's website (XThatEx.com), or just pass along certain bits of advice or information from its contents as you see fit.

No one instinctively knows what to do in these tough situations. This stuff is not coded into our DNA. Your willingness to seek out information and to be open, inquisitive, and curious about the experience of the person you are trying to support can make the difference between your being a well-intentioned but ineffective helper or a lifesaver.

▶ Don't Take It Personally

Learning more about your loved one's post-breakup world can also help soothe any ruffled feathers you may have about her not following your advice. If your loved one doesn't take your advice or takes it and then goes back on it, know that her indecision and her need to try multiple solutions—including returning to the relationship—are the norm when it comes to detaching from a manipulative Ex. A woman's inability or seeming unwillingness to follow sound advice says more about her level of stress, her Ex's manipulative strategies, or the complexity of the situation than it does about how much respect or love she has for the advice giver. In a nutshell, it isn't personal when she doesn't do what you want, even though it may feel that way. Knowing it isn't personal can help you avoid feeling like you need to resort to "tough love," punish her by keeping her at arm's length, or make her account for deviating from your advice. These reactions tend to make the situation worse. At the very least they will put her on the defensive and possibly make her more hopeless.

▶ Say It So She Can Hear It

I am not advocating that we always support our loved one's actions or turn a blind eye to certain self-destructive behaviors that are emotionally unhealthy or potentially dangerous. You deserve to have your thoughts and feelings heard, too, and talking about the logical consequences of an action or the bad outcomes you see on the horizon can be important parts of the helping process. In other words, you don't just have to stand on the sidelines wringing your hands, or be a pushover for what you see happening. What I'm saying is that *how* you show disagreement or voice your concerns is very important.

If you approach your loved one in a caring and concerned way instead of as a punishing drill sergeant demanding answers, you will be able to have a much more open conversation and possibly spur her to consider aspects of her decisions that she had not fully explored before. But you must position yourself as her ally (which you are) and give her the space within the conversation to change her mind or explain something to you that you have not considered. Express yourself in a loving way, for example, "It makes me so sad to see you struggle like this. I think the decision you are making is dangerous, and I don't understand why you have decided to do things this way." Adopting that tone gets your concerns across, opens doors to communication, and keeps you on her team. Avoid harsh, judgmental declarations like, "Aren't you ever going to get it? You make the same mistakes over and over again. Why do you have to be so damn stubborn?" Statements like these close doors and hearts.

True communication is not just about one party or the other getting their way but about the sharing and clarifying of information. And if you are able to really communicate with her, share mutual respect, and come from a place of love, no matter what decision she makes you will have done everything you can to help the outcome be the best it can be.

Mistake #2: Assuming That All Breakups Are Created Equal

Goes something like this: "I've left relationships before. It's not rocket science. She must like being treated like this."

These statements rely on an assumption that is absolutely false: that leaving a "normal" relationship is just like leaving one with a bad or manipulative Ex.

This couldn't be farther from the truth. Healthy Exes accept when their former partners say "no," they generally take responsibility for their actions, and even post-breakup, although they may be angry for some time, they end up wanting the best for the other person. When we consciously or unconsciously rely on the assumption that all breakups are alike, it can lead us to lots of wrong conclusions and to hurting the people we love. It is common for us to relate another person's experience to our own as a way of understanding it. This ability is very useful in our daily lives and often helps us to find empathy for others and solutions to all kinds of problems. But in terms of breakups, if all we have experienced is leaving normal relationships, we may or may not realize that this is a poor frame of reference for what our loved one is going through. Comparing a breakup with a difficult but emotionally healthy person to a breakup with one who is not is like comparing apples to oranges.

Differences Between Healthy Exes and Unhealthy Exes

Healthy Exes	Unhealthy Exes
Accept when their former partner says "no"	Do not accept the word "no" and will fight it
Take appropriate responsibility for their actions	Do not take responsibility for their actions and instead makes excuses
May be angry but want their former partner to be happy	Care more for their own happiness
Understand that they alone control their feelings and actions	Believe that others, including their former partner, control their actions and feelings
Will not fight dirty to get their partner to come back	Will cross the line into manipulation, tricks, and traps to get their partner to come back
Understand what love is	Think love means getting what they want or having their partner submit to their wishes
Can be reasoned with and accept compromise	Are not open to reasoning that goes against their wants, and see compromise as unacceptable

These are just some of the differences between a healthy Ex and a destructive one. *Please understand that these dissimilarities have a colossal impact on what it is like to detach and stay away from an unhealthy Ex.*

It is also true that even if you have gone through a breakup with a bad Ex, you still aren't an expert on your friend's reality. While you may have a somewhat better understanding of the situation than other folks who haven't been through it, having one bad Ex under your belt doesn't necessarily give you the full picture. Different hurtful Exes use different tactics (many of which are described in this book). They deploy these maneuvers in ways specifically calculated to impact their former partners, who are also unique individuals. These strategies are intended to break down self-esteem; create doubt; make leaving seem like a bad idea, impossible, or even dangerous; and plant the idea that if a woman will hang in there things will change. With all these variables working together, the ways your hurtful Ex acted and the impact it had on you probably differ greatly from those experienced by your loved one.

Rather than assuming you know what it's like to walk in her shoes, try the following approaches.

▶ Cut Her a Lot of Slack

If you want to comprehend what your loved one is going through, it is best to get educated on the subject of difficult or dangerous relationships, stay humble about what you may or may not know, and remain as understanding and nonjudgmental as possible.

You are also wise to remember to give your loved one the benefit of the doubt. Friends and relatives often fail to fully understand why their loved one is hesitant or fearful of cutting all ties with her Ex, or why she keeps being tempted to return. Instead of believing there is something wrong with her, or that she must in some way enjoy the treatment she receives from her Ex, I encourage you to accept the fact that you can't know everything about the situation and about the individuals involved. This means understanding that she is making the best decisions she knows how to, under incredibly difficult circumstances, and that no one likes to be treated badly.

An exception to this general rule is if you believe that a child, your loved one, or a vulnerable adult is in danger or at risk of abuse. If you have any concerns that someone may be at risk for being abused, read the sections in Chapter 3 titled "'What About the Children?'" and "'You're Going to Be Sorry'" to understand more fully your options and responsibilities for protecting the ones you love.

▶ Be on Her Side

Acting as a mouthpiece for the Ex or as a mediator for the relationship is another uninformed and very destructive choice friends and family members sometimes make. This happens when they do not understand the differences between leaving a destructive Ex and leaving a relatively healthy one. Friends and relatives cannot change or rehabilitate a bad Ex—*and neither can the woman who is leaving the relationship.* Her Ex may attempt to enlist friends and family in this effort, so be on the alert for this tactic. You can learn more about this strategy and how it harms your loved one by reading the section in Chapter 5 titled "Shut Down Friends with Messages." The best way for you to support your loved one while she's leaving a hurtful Ex is by believing her, even if you don't always fully agree with her, and by staying securely in her corner.

Remember that hurtful Exes don't usually introduce themselves to outsiders as the person they are behind closed doors. They don't meet you and say, "Hi, Christina's friend/sister/father. I am Nathan, a super-jealous and controlling guy who makes Christina feel like she isn't good enough and that she's responsible for my problems. What time is dinner?" Or, " Nice to meet you, Ashley's grandma/brother/mother. I am Marco. I regularly opt to ignore Ashley's feelings, and repeatedly belittle her in small ways only to tell her to lighten up and that I was just joking. Ashley has told me so much about you." No, the people who hurt our loved ones rarely show us their true colors, and why would they? It serves them for us to be in the dark, unaware of the full humiliation, disrespect, or mistreatment they've heaped on the person we love. Most manipulative Exes are excellent spin doctors; more often than not they will try to convince others that they are the ones who have been done wrong. Don't fall for these tricks. Your doing so will only throw one more hurdle in the path to your loved one's freedom and happiness. Instead, keep yourself squarely in her corner, and refuse to buy into her Ex's manipulations and excuses.

Mistake #3: Letting Yourself Reach the Breaking Point

Goes something like this: "I just can't take it anymore. If she says one more thing about her Ex, I'm going to scream!"

These are the words of a fed-up and emotionally overextended family member or friend. It is certainly not uncommon at some point for those providing support to a person leaving a destructive relationship to reach the end of their emotional rope. These words are often spoken self-protectively by a friend or relative, especially if that person feels burned by his or her attempts to help. They also signal the helper's need for additional boundaries with the loved one around their emotional connection and offers of help.

When the friend or relative senses that their boundaries are failing and that they are becoming overwhelmed or immobilized by their frustration, sadness, and pain, they attempt to protect themselves by shutting out the source of this discomfort, which happens to be their loved one. While this may temporarily help ease the helper's pain, it can be devastating for the loved one, who is already in a bad way. The helper may later experience feelings of guilt and regret for cutting off support. If he or she feels up to helping again but still lacks the knowledge of how to take care of him- or herself through the process, he or she may end up feeling swamped once again by the loved one's needs and by the pain of witnessing the relationship and the leaving process.

Employ the following self-care techniques *before* you've reached emotional overload, or if it feels like you're about to.

▶ Avoid the Helper-Guilt Cycle

Do your best to stay in touch with your emotions throughout the helping process, and moderate your emotional connection to certain results. For example, remove from your shoulders the unreasonable expectation that through your influence on your loved one, she will be convinced to stay away from her Ex. You do not have this power. I've seen friends and relatives get a laser-beam focus on wanting to prevent their loved one from doing certain things, like talking to or getting back together with the Ex. Then the helper is absolutely devastated if they do not get their wish.

This is completely understandable. I empathize with helpers on this issue. Still, I encourage you to avoid letting your expectations get too high or becoming too attached to specific outcomes. Believe me, there have been times when I, too, have felt brokenhearted over a woman's decision to return to her destructive Ex, or over her taking actions that place her in jeopardy of returning. These feelings of being let down, angry, or concerned can increase exponentially when you are emotionally close to the person who is struggling. It helps me to stay grounded if I maintain realistic expectations, curb my attachment to certain outcomes, and know that there is always tomorrow. I remind myself of the possibility that just because someone has taken what appears to be a step backward does not mean that all is lost or that her journey is over. Within this journey there will be highs and lows, and a helper with endurance guided by the right perspective and by balanced expectations can keep pace and make even the lows feel an awful lot better.

▶ Keep Your Balance

Helpers need to increase their own self-care and obtain support from others in order to cope effectively with the stress of being there for a loved one. This is easy to say but often difficult to do. Strategies for staying emotionally and physically balanced during this stressful time include seeking counseling, talking to trusted others about what you are going through, exercising, and eating and sleeping well. Remember, if you fail to take care of yourself and to maintain your own emotional balance, your ability to be a support for your loved one will be impaired. Self-sacrifice for another's well-being is an amazing thing, but only up to a certain point. You have to keep your own boat afloat if you hope to help prevent others from drowning.

As part of your strategy for avoiding becoming overwhelmed, you may need to set small, medium, or large boundaries with your loved one along the way. These limits will need to take into account whether you're feeling emotionally overextended or unbalanced, or if what is being asked of you goes against your best judgment of what is healthy. Here's an example of a small boundary: It is the third night she has called you at midnight crying about something her Ex said, and you tell her you are tired and need to wait until the morning to talk. A medium-size boundary may require telling her that you cannot be the one to assist her in moving her things away from his house, perhaps because you need to go to work or you choose to support her in other ways. Setting a large boundary may involve kindly telling her that she cannot move in with you because you tried that before and it just didn't work. You may need to set all these limits and many more. Certainly you want to do so gently. By putting these parameters into place you will increase your ability to help over the long term rather than burning out.

▶ Be a Myth Breaker

Many of us harbor an unexamined belief in society's myths about breakups, and in giving advice to our loved one we may rely on them instead of thinking carefully about the type of authentic care she deserves. Popular but usually untrue cultural messages about relationships abound, for example: "A breakup can be just the thing to whip a man into shape." "Give him another chance, because love conquers all." "If a man fights a breakup it means he really loves you." Mindlessly repeating clichés such as these to someone who is leaving a destructive relationship can spell disaster for her attempts to break free.

Instead of parroting these common myths, do some soul searching about what words you can use to help alleviate the guilt, pain, and judgments your loved one may be facing—from both herself and others. Statements like, "You are a good person and didn't deserve to be treated that way," "He had no right to do that to you," and "I know you did everything you could" are antidotes to our culture's harmful breakup myths. They can help relieve the unfair pressure that is sometimes heaped on women who are separating from bad Exes. For more information on these harmful but all-too-common myths, please read "Breaking Up Breakup Myths," page 128.

◀ ▶

Remember that leaving a destructive Ex is almost always a long process, not a quick event. As I said toward the beginning of this book, staying away from a destructive Ex is like a marathon, requiring incredible perseverance and stamina. Perhaps the majority of women will return at least once to a destructive Ex. That is just the nature of the beast, and it is a scenario bad Exes often work hard to perpetuate. It does not mean that these women are somehow broken, poor decision makers, or at fault. Women who leave destructive relationships are often under huge pressures. They must make due with what little our society offers them in the way of support, options, and even safety.

In stark contrast, you are willing to give something of yourself to help make possible your loved one's dream of lasting separation from her Ex. What a miracle. Your backing during this tumultuous time may be the most selfless and important gift you ever give, and it may be the most crucial one she will ever receive. If you want to be able to support your loved one over the long haul, you must take care of yourself, pay attention to your boundaries and emotional well-being, and avoid unintentionally harmful actions. I wish you good luck, and I and many others are grateful for your sacrifice.

Index